Collection Conundrums
Solving Collections Management Mysteries

Rebecca A. Buck and Jean Allman Gilmore

AMERICAN ASSOCIATION OF MUSEUMS

© 2007 American Association of Museums
1575 Eye St. N.W., Suite 400
Washington, DC 20005

Design: Design35

On the cover: *Cabinet of the Terrestrial Realm* from Mark Dion's "Cabinet of Curiosities."
Weisman Art Museum, Minneapolis, February 24–May 27, 2001.
Photo by Robert Fogt.

Library of Congress Cataloging-in-Publication Data

Buck, Rebecca A., 1946-
 Collection conundrums : solving collections management mysteries / Rebecca
A. Buck and Jean Allman Gilmore.
     p. cm.
 Includes bibliographical references and index.
 ISBN 978-1-933253-08-4 (alk. paper)
 1. Museums--Collection management. I. Gilmore, Jean Allman, 1946- II.
American Association of Museums. III. Title.

AM133.B83 2007
069'.5--dc22

2007010294

Collection Conundrums

Contents

Acknowledgments

Standards and procedures are developed over time by many people within the museum profession. In order to represent what collections staff do and outline solutions that might be best for a variety of museum collections issues, we have relied on numerous people: registrars, curators, collection managers, directors, lawyers, teachers and students. Panels at professional conferences offer clues, as do the myriad questions and responses on listservs. Museum professionals have proven to be open and positive in their advice and in sharing their resources, and all of those who have discussed thorny collections issues have moved the process forward.

For this publication, Ildiko DeAngelis has written about old loans and reviewed the legal issues to help us be certain we were on track; her students at George Washington University developed the basic legal reference chart. Douglas F. Browne, a lawyer who is not directly involved with museums in his work, also studied the legal issues and offered direction for reference. Douglas J. Robinson, who worked with such diligence on the third edition of *Museum Registration Methods*, graciously shared his expertise and experience. Holly Young wrote and offered moral support.

Many thanks go to the staff of the Eastern Washington State Historical Society's Northwest Museum of Arts and Culture (MAC), especially Larry Schoonover, Laura Thayer and Rose Krause, for their kindness and help in developing a case study on solving collections problems. Larry, recently retired, was a great mentor and has worked long to make the MAC a museum of excellence.

Pamela M. Hensen, historian at the Smithsonian Institution Archives, helped track the history of registrars, as did Adrianna Del Collo at the Metropolitan Museum of Art archives. Katie Speckart shared her lecture on methods of finding lenders and helped clarify several "Found in Collection" (FIC) issues. Melinda Simms was generous in sharing her work on FIC objects completed as part of the John F. Kennedy University Masters in Museum Studies program. Linda Wilhelm was generous with images; Jeanne Benas, registrar of the National Museum of American History, served as a reader, also clarifying FIC. David Ryan is responsible for the Colorado Springs Pioneer Museum sidebar on relics in museum collection. Louise LaPlante discussed university loan collections and Timothy Decker helped with ephemera. Ted Greenberg researched community property in California, and several registrars, Stephen Ringle in particular, helped with definitions. Tyra Walker and Pam West, regional curator in charge of the national Vietnam Veterans

Memorial, and Katie Witzig, collections manager of the New Jersey Vietnam Veterans Memorial, shared information about institutions with large collections of memorials.

Several people helped with research and direction: Maureen Harper (NERA workshop material); Elizabeth B. Merritt (American Association of Museums' history); Marie Demeroukas (Arkansas law); Lynn Swain (Delaware law); Leslie Orly Lewellen (loan forms); Jennifer Bottomly-O'Looney (Montana law); and Suzanne Quigley (New York law). The Newark Museum librarian, William Peniston, and archivist, Jeffrey Moy, were instrumental in finding the research material needed for sections on history, and Ulysses Grant Dietz, curator of decorative arts, was clear on the subject of ephemera. Newark colleagues Batja Bell, Amber Germano, Heidi Warbasse, Scott Hankins and Greg Bugel offered advice and comments along the way. Virginia O'Hara, curator of collections, Brandywine River Museum, wrote about finding people on the Internet.

A group formed through the Registrars Committee listserv acted as a sounding board during the process. Thanks to James Burns, Debbie Garcia, Deborah Cooper, Dorren Martin-Ross, Linda Wilhelm, Melinda Simms, Rosemary Sallee, Stephen Lockwood, Virginia Pifko and Maureen McCormick. Antonia Moser, Michelle Budenz and Alana Cole-Faber, students in the Seton Hall Museum Professions program, read and discussed several parts of the manuscript as well.

The Newark Museum and the Brandywine River Museum were supportive as we worked through the issues of this book. Many thanks to Mary Sue Sweeney Price, director, and Meme Omogbai, chief operating officer of the Newark Museum, and to James H. Duff, executive director of the Brandywine River Museum. Ward L. E. Mintz, formerly of the Newark Museum, worked with John Sare to help us get legal assistance as research was undertaken.

Our AAM editor, Lisa Meyerowitz, who came to the project late in its life, handled the manuscript skillfully and efficiently; it has been a pleasure to work with her and with John Strand of the American Association of Museums staff. We would also like to thank Christiane Riederer von Paar and Claudia Bohn-Spector of Design35 for their clean and elegant design. Jim Reuter and G. L. Gilmore have once more wondered at our interest in rather quiet and obscure issues, but have been tolerant of our efforts. Thanks, guys!

Rebecca A. Buck
Jean Allman Gilmore

1: Introduction, History, Terminology

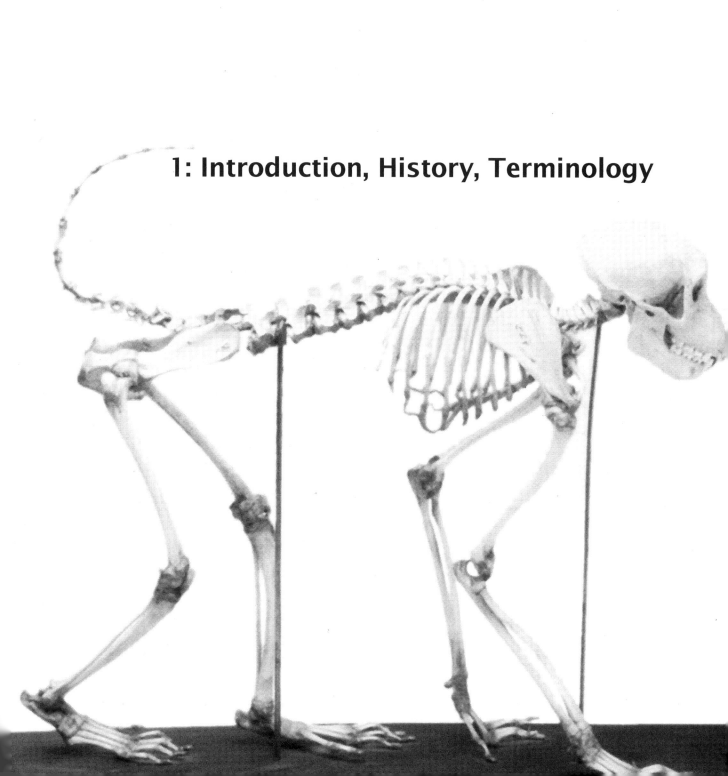

All objects are equal but some are more equal than others . . .

PUBLIC TRUST

The permanent collections of a museum form the core of the institution. They rise from the mission, they inform the programs and they shape the direction of the institution. If a museum adheres to professional standards, care is taken with everything that is done with them. The well-managed museum provides sophisticated environmental systems, good security, safe exhibition techniques and storage systems that minimize threat to the physical safety of the collection. It takes care to pack, crate and ship collection objects in the best possible way to avoid damage. Its documentation procedures are complex, thorough and geared to tracking the physical integrity and presenting the correct intellectual attributes of each object.

The laws that define governmental museums and those that regulate private museums are complex and change from state to state.[1] Unless museums are commercial (Madame Tussauds Wax Museum, for example), their collections are held for the benefit of the public. Oversight of this public trust in each state rests in the office of the attorney general. The responsibility for care of the collections is guided by law and by the higher professional and ethical standards set by professional organizations. The American Association of Museums, as the organization that accredits American museums, works constantly to upgrade standards and promote excellence.

THE ACCESSIONED OBJECT

When an object enters a museum's permanent collection, its status changes. There is no more drinking from the cup, no more playing with the doll, no more never-ending display for the watercolor. Housing and environmental issues alien to the object's origin and initial use loom large, and a pedestal awaits for future exhibition. The object, by virtue of the fact that it has been "accessioned,"[2] is accorded higher value than its counterparts on the

The Perfect Accessioned Object: 26.2755, Hiram Powers, *The Greek Slave*, 1847. The Newark Museum, gift of Franklin Murphy, Jr., 1926.

outside. Usually there is no question that the accessioned object deserves this higher esteem.

Museum professionals often idealize the accessioned object while at the same time overlooking the fact that many accessioned objects do not meet the standard. Accessioning is an equalizer for objects within a museum collection. To collections staff, all accessioned objects must be treated in accordance with professional practices that have been transformed into institutional policy and procedure. The standards and best practices for collections care and documentation, which are outlined in texts, taught in museum studies courses and discussed in professional meetings and publications, must be applied equally.

Museum professionals acknowledge problems arising from old collecting and documentation practices, discuss them at length and attempt to formulate solutions but usually have insufficient staff and legal counsel available to pursue resolution. A tension builds between objects of great value and insignificant objects with little relevance to the museum's mission, between objects clearly owned by the museum and those of shadowy status.[3] Since an object of lesser value is more likely to have unclear status than an object of greater value, the bottom end of the scale becomes increasingly murky. Objects vie for space, care and the time that must be spent to document and resolve issues surrounding them. The lesser objects take away space and time from the greater, and the needs of the greater preclude care, documentation and subsequent disposition of the lesser.

After time, objects of unclear status take on the attributes of the accessioned object. A museum staff member may have given them a number. They are in storage with like objects and may have catalogue cards or some makeshift documentation. They appear on inventories and are given tracking numbers. In essence, they must be treated according to the standards of collection objects until their stories can be sorted out and they can be either disassociated from or made more clearly a part of the permanent collection.

When human nature mixes with chronic lack of space, too few collections staff and informal collecting histories, museums face some form of this problem. Its manifestations include accessioned objects that are not useful to the museum, partially accessioned objects, found-in-collection objects, old loans, deaccessioned objects never discarded, wrongly accessioned property, abandoned property and special supplemental collections. Throw in a few institutional transfers, some special event decorations and a reproduction returned as an object from a white elephant sale or give-away from the past, and the mix becomes extremely difficult to sort out. These problems are not unique to history museums, nor to general museums. Any museum may find itself dealing with one or many of these situations.

In the ideal world there are no lesser objects, nor objects of uncertain status, among the accessioned. Kudos to any museum that has managed to keep its permanent collection clear of such felonies and high misdemeanors! The ideal product of collections policies and practices is to make all accessioned objects within a collection equal. The objects in a museum collection should be in tune with the mission of the museum; they should be of value to the programs that the museum generates and they should all merit the expense of care, documentation, housing, environment and conservation. This does not mean that all objects must be treated to exactly the same measure of care during storage, loan or exhibition. The history, value, fragility and material components of the objects determine that level. It is not at all unusual to have million-dollar paintings, a local haberdasher's box, a mammoth's tooth and an 1860s salt crock in the same collection. They become equal when they are all valuable to the museum and are all treated with the highest standard of care determined by type of object.

In order to resolve the problems caused by uneven collecting practices and take control of collections, there must be a two-pronged attack. First, every museum should follow clear policies that lead to high-quality collections additions with clear title. A concerted attempt must be made to keep all strange material and borderline objects out of the collection. Do not put the city award plaque in the collection; think it through and add it to the institutional archive. Tell the founder's daughter that trinkets from Tasmania do not matter to a museum with regional historical interests. That bad portrait of the mayor does not belong in the art collection. Keep loan records current. Keep the accessioning process up-to-date. Plan and perform inventories, and resolve historical problems whenever possible.

Second, museums must find ways to resolve problems arising from the hazy collecting practices of the past. Many museums have instituted procedures that help them sort out old loans, undocumented objects and supplementary collections. There is not, however, a body of literature for American museums who wish to undertake processes to clarify collection status without reinventing the wheel. It is with the hope of solidifying some standards already in place and encouraging discussion of others that this book was begun.

It may seem fairly simple to resolve collection issues, but it is not. It may seem even simpler to prevent them. Again, it is not. Many museums, particularly small institutions without professional staff, continue to invent the legal and practical procedures they believe they should follow. Some replicate the informal procedures of the early part of the twentieth century, accepting material without review, using oral contracts or small handwritten notes. Some accept material without paying attention to the mission of the museum and the practical considerations of taking care of that material in the future. It is not unusual to find a fairly new museum with no idea of the extent of its collections and no proof of ownership of those collections. The enthusiastic individuals who create museums are often more visionary than practical—they are directors and curators, not registrars and collections managers. They do not have staff to balance the vision with the practical concerns. Other museums fold in entire collections from defunct museums and inherit all of the issues that existed in the former institution.

Established museums with staff generally try, especially since the American Association of Museums (AAM) instituted their accreditation program in 1971, to keep problems from occurring in their collections. They also are aware of many of the solutions to problems they have inherited. Some museums have undertaken major projects to clarify title and claim old loans. More museums, however, have not been able to spend the time necessary to review and organize collections completely. In order to understand the problems' origins, and to begin to look for solutions, it is important to know something of the history of collection development and the standards for collection documentation and care.

HISTORY OF COLLECTING AND DEVELOPMENT OF STANDARDS

Many of the first museums of the United States started with collections of scientific and natural history specimens; this was a direct outgrowth of museums of curios and natural history specimens in Europe. Some of these—such as the Charleston Museum of Charleston, South Carolina—flourished

from the late 1700s. In New Hampshire, Dartmouth College traces its collecting history to a donation of money in 1772 for the acquisition of "philosophical apparatus." On October 26, 1772, Reverend David McClure wrote to Reverend Eleazar Wheelock, president of Dartmouth: "I have collected a few curious Elephants Bones found about six hundred miles down the Ohio, for the young Museum of Dartmouth, which I shall forward to Philadelphia the first conveyance."[4] One of the specimens he sent is still extant in the collection of Dartmouth's Hood Museum of Art.

772.1.30192, Mammoth tooth. Courtesy of the Hood Museum of Art, Dartmouth College, Hanover, New Hampshire, gift of David McClure.

Most of the early museums were established in the northeastern part of the country. The Peabody Essex Museum in Salem, Massachusetts, was founded in 1799. The Pennsylvania Academy of the Fine Arts began in Philadelphia in 1805, and later, from 1822 through 1828, Peale's Museum of natural history specimens was installed in Independence Hall. That museum moved to Baltimore and was later destroyed by fire. Back in New England, Yale developed its first museum in New Haven, Connecticut, in 1832 and the Wadsworth Atheneum Museum of Art was founded in Hartford, Connecticut, in 1842.

Frederick A. Lucas, curator-in-chief, Museum of the Brooklyn Institute of Arts and Sciences, in his 1907 paper, entitled "The Evolution of Museums," published the following year, discusses the changes that took place from the earliest museums through the end of the nineteenth century:

Thus museums have passed through several distinct states; at first they were indiscriminate gatherings of curios, objects of art, and specimens of natural history. Then, by the inevitable process of segregation, natural history came to have a place by itself, the collections of scientific societies developed as storehouses of material, mainly for the use of the specialist and the public museums derived from these were largely dryly scientific in their character.

In terms of use and content, museums moved from cabinets of curiosities held by individuals to collections that represented specific disciplines. Lucas lamented the number of curiosities that remained in museums of the United States at the turn of the century:

[A] vast number of objects were of that class rightly called curiosities, a comprehensive term that embraces a vast and miscellaneous category of objects, including the familiar and ever-present petrified potato and four-legged chicken. If there is anything that a museum has no use and no place for, it is the mere curiosity, but, as John Minto says in a recent article, "It will take years to do away with the idea of museums still entertained by many that they are storehouses of curiosities."[5]

Many museums do retain curios as part of the history of collecting, to graphically illustrate historical events and even, at times, to put local events into a greater context.

The Charleston Museum's telephone answering recording welcomes callers to "America's first museum, founded in 1773." The museum was closed for a few days during the Revolutionary War and again during an evacuation caused by the Civil War, but otherwise it has remained open. Over the years it collected natural history and ethnology, and in the 1900s it began collecting material culture. The age and nature of the collections makes it impossible truly to count the objects, which are estimated to be in the millions. A justified inventory is even more difficult, since the first systematic accession ledger was not put in place until around 1902.

That first ledger, and the extended system it represented, was discussed at the 1907 meeting of AAM in Pittsburgh, Pennsylvania, by Paul M. Rea, then director of the Charleston Museum. It was devised, he said, to meet the conditions of "extensive collections . . . the accumulations of more than a century . . . data, scattered on loose labels and in old memorandum books, [which] had to be associated with their specimens. . . ." The first of those books was from 1798. In 1902 the museum put in place a four-part record system to control its collections: an accession ledger, with sequential numbers from one to infinity, representing lots; specimen records with unique numbers for each specimen that were then placed on the specimen; a finding list with numbers, specimen name and location; and a list of sources.

Henry Watson Kent developed a business system for Metropolitan Museum of Art accessions around 1905. In 1907 Lucas stated that

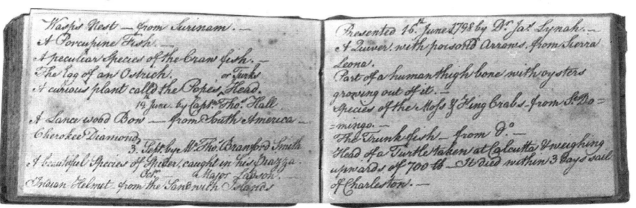

Page from a 1798 ledger. Courtesy of the Charleston Museum, Charleston, South Carolina.

collections should not be made haphazardly, that they should have definite purposes and that collections should form a consistent whole (see p. 8). The first surge of standardization was underway, and with the founding of AAM in 1906 and its first full presentations of papers in 1907, professionalism for museum workers was formally launched in the United States.

During the ensuing years many museums were founded, and sometimes museums were developed with careful choices and carefully crafted systems for collecting, collections care and collections documentation. Often, though, wheels were reinvented and curios or uncontrolled collections were the order of the day.

Early collection control systems evolved from prototypes found in the world of libraries, and no major breakthroughs in museum documentation and object tracking methods occurred until computer database programs became commonplace in the 1990s. There were, however, some developments toward the systems that are currently most popular. Museums first used the simple sequential system employed by libraries in their accession ledgers—1, 2, 3, 4, 5—to number lots of objects. By 1909, two-part systems came into use. Some museums bypassed the idea of the accession as a group and applied sequential object numbers in each year, e.g., 9.1, 9.2, 9.3 for the first three objects in 1909, whether or not from the same source. By 1927 there is evidence of the three-part system in some museums: 27.1.1 marks the first object of the first accession of 1927. Such registration evolution has created many of the collection control problems museums now face. It resulted in inconsistent systems within institutions. Museums might have two or three, or in some cases, even fifteen different systems in place. They might have used the three-part system and gone back and forth between that and other systems. Confusion still abounds.

Libraries standardized documentation and care because they could: they deal primarily with multiples that can be easily catalogued and to a great extent homogeneous materials that are eas-

ily housed, and they do not have stringent restrictions on disposing of material. Museums, on the other hand, contend with mastodon skeletons and pinned bugs, with huge sculptures and miniature paintings. They must accommodate high value and unique objects, and an ever-strengthening ethic to use great care and trustee review when disposing of objects.

Some museum collections problems arise from the interactions of great egos. Scholars base career advancement on publications and presentations grounded in collection pieces. Collectors want to showcase their knowledge and wealth and be recognized as benefactors to museums. Trustees, almost always successful businessmen and women and community leaders, often have risen to their places in society because of their assertiveness, clarity and eventual wealth. There are many instances where museums are left with rooms of objects that must be displayed together, according to the wishes of the original collector and donor. There are stories of curators whose prowess in fieldwork was so strong that the incidental personal collection of a thousand toys was accepted without a murmur in order to assure the continued collecting of native artifacts. In short, the world of museums is a world of strong characters.

During its first fifty years, AAM worked to establish standards for the care and use of museum permanent collections and to apply those standards, as needed, to museum activities other than accessions. AAM's first code of ethics, called Code of Ethics for Museum Workers, dates to 1925. Loans became a popular way to develop broader exhibitions than a single museum could do alone. When it became obvious that loans had to be monitored, museums came together and devised procedures to do that.

The decade of the 1950s was vital in the development of standards for collections care, and it culminated in the publication of *Museum Registration Methods* in 1958. The book was written by Dorothy H. Dudley, registrar at the Museum of Modern Art in New York, and Irma

Bezold, later Irma Wilkinson, registrar at the Metropolitan Museum of Art. They were joined by a diverse group of registrars, administrators and conservators, including Geraldine Bruckner, registrar at the University Museum, University of Pennsylvania; Richard D. Buck, conservator at the Intermuseum Laboratory in Oberlin, Ohio; and David B. Little, secretary-registrar of the Museum of Fine Arts, Boston. AAM proclaimed its stance on collection care in the foreword, written by AAM president William M. Milliken:

The American Association of Museums is deeply concerned with the question of standards in the museums it serves. One of its main purposes is to place the career of the museum employee upon the highest possible professional level, and to do this it has from time to time issued publications which bear upon one or another of the many problems which concerns museums, large or small. One of the most fundamental of them is the basic function of the Registrar.

The vitality of the Association depends increasingly upon its usefulness and the cooperation of its members. The Registrars as a group have recognized this and by united action they have prepared the essential information which is contained in this important volume.

The position of registrar in American museums dates at least from 1880 when Stephen C. Brown, an assistant in the division of reptiles at the National Museum, was named first registrar of the Smithsonian Institution. A reference in Henry Watson Kent's memoir, *What I Am Pleased to Call My Education*, indicates that the title "registrar" was in use by 1906 in art museums. Patrick Reynolds, an assistant curator, became the first registrar at the Metropolitan Museum of Art in that year. Kent says "The Registrar . . . carried a Latin Bible in his pocket, from which he would ask you to read passages, to test your scholarship." By 1925, there was a registrar's job description at the Newark Museum. A title like secretary or secretary-registrar meant

an administrative position, not simply a clerical one. Henry Watson Kent, assistant secretary at the Metropolitan, for example, held a highly placed position concerned with policy-making. He used the term "business methods" to explain accessioning procedures and described taking over the records of the museum from General Cesnola's secretary, saying that they were "docketed in the old-fashioned way and bound up with red tape," noting that his job was to "catalogue and file them in new-fashioned cases of Dewey's devising." His position was thoroughly professional and built on a career as librarian and museum director.

Newark Museum Registrar

John Cotton Dana, director of the Newark Museum, outlined the duties of museum registrar in April 1925 as follows:

a. Registry and care of collection: combination of schedules of registrar and assistant.

b. Receive, record, accession, label, store and follow up all gifts, purchases and loans: prepare and list objects for storage warehouse: care for all storage and working equipment within the building.

c. File and care for all labels and posters, replace soiled ones.

d. Care of photos and negatives: accessioning, mounting, labeling, filing.

e. Books, etc. in Museum library: periodicals, record and binding: catalogue, shelve, inventory.

f. Color band files of trade and exhibit catalogues.

g. Exhibitions, particularly physical care of objects on exhibition.

Some Business Methods in the Metropolitan Museum of Art

Henry Watson Kent, Assistant Secretary, Metropolitan Museum of Art
From *Proceedings of the American Association of Museums* vol. 6, Records of the Sixth Annual Meeting Held at Boston, Mass., May 23–25, 1911, pp. 31–34.

Under the constitution of the museum of which I shall speak, like other museums of its kind, no doubt, the action upon the bequest, gift, or purchase of objects of art is taken by the trustees sitting in committees and approved by the entire board. This necessitates a system of business in the executive offices which, with as little loss of time and energy as possible, shall be thorough and all-informing. I may use this expression to mean the notification of a given action to all concerned—donor, vendor, curator, treasurer, registrar, photographer, sales department, and daily press. At just what point legitimate business methods become red tape has never been clearly defined, but doubtless a business house would place it where system ceases to show a profit. Surely neither such red tape nor slipshod unbusinesslike methods of administration should be tolerated in a museum any more than in a factory, although this is a point which does not seem to have been considered worthy of much attention heretofore, if we judge from the literature on the subject.

By some, a system, which in the telling may seem complicated, may be deemed unnecessary, but when it is remembered that in a large museum many different persons are affected by a single transaction, that the physical safety of the object is an important consideration in a building of long distances where many employees and visitors are coming and going, that thousands of objects are added in a year, and that hundreds of thousands of dollars are involved in these transactions, it will be seen that a careful and unvarying system must take the place of haphazard communications.

In the following statement I shall endeavor to explain a system which has been found to be necessary to meet the needs both of the executive offices and of those persons whose work is governed by the action of the trustees.

Gifts and bequests are usually offered by letter. This, when acknowledged by the secretary, is copied and sent to the chairman of the committee of the trustees concerned with the statement that the objects offered will be examined by the director and the curator in whose department they would be included if accepted, and that a report of their recommendation will be sent to him later. The donor or representative of an estate is informed that the gift of bequest will be acted upon by the trustees at their next meeting. Copies of the original letter are furnished to the director and the curator, who, after the object has been sent to the Museum, draw up their reports upon blank forms furnished by the secretary, which with other similar forms are sent to the chairman before the meeting of his committee.

If the object is accepted by trustees upon the committee's recommendation, a suitable acknowledgement is sent to the donor. Notification of this action is sent by the secretary to the curator and to the registrar, who will already have received the object, giving a temporary receipt for it. At the time of the receipt of the object, the registrar sends to the secretary a card called from its color "the blue card," upon which he notes as much information concerning the thing itself as has come under his observation. The return of this card, filled in with additional data furnished by the curator, serves as his notification of the trustees' action. The registrar then accessions the object in a volume which follows in its general arrangement the accession book perfected by libraries. The use of this kind of record, by the way, is rapidly being discontinued by the libraries that first adopted it and it is questionable whether the time spent upon it in museums is not unnecessary. The registrar numbers the accession, his numbers running consecutively under the numeral indicating the year, and sends it to the photographer along with the blue card, keeping a copy for himself. Thus the blue card becomes what express companies call a "tracer." The object is photographed in as many sizes as the importance of the subject, the needs of the sales department, and the demands of registration and cataloguing may require. When the photographs are made, the negative is registered by the photographer, the number of it being added to the blue card along with a print four by five inches which is pasted on the back, and both object and card are then returned to the registrar. The card is then filed in the order of the accession book entry, the record being now completed by the photograph, and object itself is delivered to the curator, who, receipting for it, thenceforth becomes responsible for its safe-keeping and display.

The system connected with purchases is somewhat more complicated since objects of this sort are of two kinds, those which are offered unsolicited and those which are brought to the attention of the trustees by the curators who desire their purchase. All objects offered for purchased are passed upon by the curator and the director, each of whom gives his recommendations on a blank form prepared in the secretary's office from information supplied from the vendor's letter or by the registrar, if the object is sent to the Museum on approval. Few of these unsolicited objects, however, are brought to the attention of the committee on purchases, because they are usually undesirable. In the course of a month, fifty such letters on the average, are acted upon without recourse to the committee. The objects recommended for purchase by the curators and the director are brought to the committee by the secretary, who after

the meeting indicates to curator, registrar, and treasurer what action has been taken. The system of notification for the first two officers is the same as for gifts. To the last officer, a card is sent giving facts connected with the purchase, such as the price to be paid, and the fund out of which it is to be paid. This card with others of its kind, arranged by classes, serves as the treasurer's voucher and aids him in making the correct entry in his books. The card remains in his office as an index to his ledgers.

While the blue card of accepted objects is still in the secretary's office, its information is rearranged on a white card—so much of it, at least, as is needed—and this is submitted to the curator for his emendations and corrections, when it becomes a catalogue entry for the new accession. Classed according to a system of classification, and with a photograph of the object pasted on its verso, it is filed in a general catalogue. Copies of this card are given to the curator of the department to which the objects belongs, who in this way secures a catalogue of his own collection. From this card is made the "copy" used by the printer in making labels.

The usefulness of the blue card is not confined to the service which has been described. Unlike the proverbial rolling stone which gathered nothing in its career, the blue card accumulates data as it travels from department to department. Besides what has been enumerated, it furnishes information to the photographer for his records to the sales department for its catalogue and labels. It gives to the Bulletin its list of monthly accessions, and to the annual report its long list of the year's acquisitions.

An account of this system is given here not because it is considered a perfect one, but in the hope that it may be suggestive to other museums and, also, in order that it may provoke such criticism as may be helpful in its perfection. It is written down in order that it may serve as a record for any new museum about to grapple with the problems of organization.

"A Piece of the True Cross: Relics and Oddities," An Exhibition from the Colorado Springs Pioneers Museum

With thanks to David Ryan, who provided this label from the Colorado Springs Pioneers Museum.

Throughout history relics have been important parts of human life. The word relic means, "something left behind," and is typically used to describe collected objects that survive from the past.

Relics create powerful and sometimes spiritual links to the past. History is often an abstract and difficult notion full of dates, names and places, however, tangible objects provide us with physical evidence of earlier times. Beyond serving as mementos, they also indicate what people value about their own history. In this way, they can be very personal and intimate.

Typically, relics are objects collected because of a special significance or specific importance to the collector. Many are said to have belonged to someone famous, or are tied to an important historical event. They often have a religious significance and are sometimes possessions or actual body parts of saints. Despite the fact that they were often of questionable origin, these items were exhibited in churches, and visited and revered by believers. For this reason, the phrase "a piece of the True Cross" is often used to describe these objects.

In earlier times American museums focused on collecting these types of "curiosities." They were eager to display exotic, foreign and unusual items as well as objects relating to national and world events. Modern museums no longer strive to collect relics in this sense, preferring to save only items that relate to a specific collecting mission and with more easily proven history (i.e., provenance).

A wide variety of relics from the Museum's collection are featured here. Some are specifically relevant to local people and places, such as the Antler's Hotel fire. Others represent national and international incidents, such as the piece of wood flooring from the White House or the Trans-Atlantic cable. Only some of these objects can be factually proven to be what they are stated. Instead, their real value is found in the beliefs that their collectors placed in them, and in the power of historical objects to evoke such strong feelings.

Plates, October 8, 1871. Colorado Springs Pioneers Museum, gift of Carlos L. Smith, 55.153.

This stack of plates was in the Chicago Fire of 1871, which burned for 27 hours. The plates were heated to the point where the glaze melted, and fused the plates together. The fire destroyed 17,450 buildings and other property valued at $196,000,000. Two-hundred fifty people died and almost 100,000 people were left homeless.

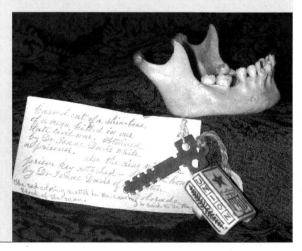

These rings [opposite, below] were carved from the shinbone of a man killed in the Civil War. Prisoners-of-war often carved to pass the time in the prisons, and as carving material was scarce, utilized anything they could get their hands on. This included human bone. The red coloring in the carving on the ring is said to be the blood of the man, however it is unlikely that blood would remain so brightly colored.

Bessie Bouton's lower jawbone is a relic of the first murder case ever to be solved using dental identification. The murder and the identification occurred here in Colorado Springs in 1904. Her jawbone was used as police evidence.

Tar and Feathers, June 23, 1894. Colorado Springs Pioneers Museum, gift of Colorado Springs Police Department, 71.166.2.

Adjutant Tarsney of the State Militia was sent by the Governor to help put an end to the violence in Cripple Creek. Unfortunately, he was kidnapped by the mob, taken north of town and tarred and feathered. This bit of the tar and feathers used on him was police evidence.

—*Courtesy of the Colorado Springs*

◄*Carved Bone Rings and Key, c. 1865.* Colorado Springs Pioneers Museum, gift of Carlos L. Smith, 55.117. *Jawbone of Bessie Bouton,* 1904. Colorado Springs Pioneers Museum, gift of the Colorado Springs Police Department, 71.181.1.

In the 1950s, registrars and their standards became more focused, and their community continued to develop. *Museum Registration Methods* was revised and published again in 1968. The scene was set for the major jump in training and professionalization that occurred in the late 1960s and early 1970s. Accreditation, a hallmark of a professional institution and of a profession, was in the making.

That jump was precipitated by the popularity of museums (by 1967 there were 5,000 museums in the United States) and the finances needed to make them run well. Museums sought federal support from newly created endowments for the arts and humanities. In order to be trusted with public monies, museums needed an accreditation system to assure the federal grant givers of the standard of stewardship in individual museums. President Lyndon B. Johnson formed a commission to study museums, and in 1968 he received the Belmont report: "The Condition and Needs of American Museums," which led directly to AAM's accreditation program. In 1971, 16 museums received accreditation.

Belmont Report

The 2005 *Museum Accreditation Handbook* offers the following explanation:

Plans for museum accreditation began in earnest in 1967 when President Lyndon B. Johnson asked the U. S. Federal Council on the Arts and Humanities to conduct a study of the status of American museums and recommend ways to support and strengthen them. The council enlisted AAM's assistance and in 1968 the association established a committee to study the idea of an accreditation program for museums. Based on AAM's input, on November 25, 1968, the council issued *America's Museums: The Belmont Report,* which stated: "It is urgent that the American Association of Museums and its member institutions develop and agree upon acceptable criteria and methods of accrediting museums."

THE NEWARK MUSEUM'S STAFF

Here is a list of the workers in this Museum, with a statement of the duties of each one. These duties are of course not as closely defined as the words used seem to indicate; and they overlap in many cases.

The list suggests the many and varied kinds of work that must be pursued even in a small museum and one that is relatively quite modest in its collections and in its assured income.

April, 1925.   J. C. D.

I. **Curator.** Responsible to Assistant Director and Director.
   A. Administration of Museum: policy and methods.
   B. Exhibitions: selection, plans and installation.
   C. Publicity: clubs and societies, other museums, news items, securing gifts and loans, etc.
   D. Purchases and equipment: follow up sales: round out collections, etc.

II. **General Assistant** in charge of office. Responsible to Curator.
   A. Give assistance to and carry out instructions of Curator.
   B. Immediate supervision and direction (schedules, routine, general duties) of office staff, attendants, janitor, science assistant; storage in warehouse.
   C. General care of rooms, property, exhibitions, storage. Paint, glass, cases, damage, etc., noted by daily inspection.
   D. Special exhibits. e. g. Chinese Traveling Exhibits. Leather show, until taken over by special worker.
   E. Preliminary preparation of meetings and minutes thereof.
   F. Correspondence.
   G. Index museum minutes; keep to date.
   H. Prepare on request: budgets and financial statements, catalogs, reports.
   I. Revision and weeding of all files: particularly correspondence and information.
   J. Indicate all filing.

III. **Registrar.** Registry and care of collections: combination of schedules of Registrar and assistant.
   A. Receive, record, accession, label, store and follow up all gifts, purchases and loans: prepare and list objects for storage warehouse: care for all storage and working equipment within the building.
   B. File and care for all labels and posters, replace soiled ones.
   C. Care of photos and negatives: accessioning, mounting, labeling, filing.
   D. Books, etc., in Museum library: periodicals, record and binding; catalog, shelve, inventory.
   E. Color band files of trade and exhibit catalogs.
   F. Exhibitions, particularly physical care of objects on exhibition.

IV. **Stenographers and office assistants:** 2 persons.
   A. Dictation (all).
   B. Typing: gift lists and form letter (quarterly), membership lists, form letters, notices, cards, minutes, etc.
   C. Filing.
   D. Stock: care and distribution as needed.
   E. Care and distribution of all museum publications, stock and other printed matter.
   F. Mailing list: keep mailing stencils for addressing machine up to date.
   G. Cuts: records, care, filing, follow-up.
   H. Attendance records.
   I. Care of desks and desk supplies (asst. in charge, curator).
   J. Cash box and stamps.
   K. Monthly bills and bill list.

V. **Lending Collections:** 3 persons.
   A. Direction and supervision: records of collections, and catalog of collections.
   B. Prepare new material, write labels and give general assistance.
   C. Fill requests, pack and unpack, file, circulation records, notices, etc., clean and repair.

VI. **Miscellaneous and special:** 3 persons.
   A. In charge of cash box and monthly preparation of bills. Supervision of such membership records as are handled in office.
   B. Museum accounts and bookkeeping. Membership and membership bills.
   C. Club activities.

◄John Cotton Dana, *Job Descriptions at the Newark Museum, 1925.* Courtesy of the Newark Museum.

The process of accreditation accelerated everything professional in museums, including the creation of more positions for collection managers, collection technicians, exhibition managers, registrars and curators. There was a growing demand for museum training programs, which had begun early in the century with courses at Harvard and an apprentice program started in the 1920s at the Newark Museum. The Cooperstown Graduate Program, founded in 1964 by Dr. Louis C. Jones, then director of the New York State Historical Association, was positioned to train professional staff for the growing number of history museums. The Winterthur Program in Early American Culture, established in 1952 to foster connoisseurship, was joined in 1972 by the University of Delaware's museum studies program to train professionals in other areas of museum and collections management. The John F. Kennedy University museum studies program in San Francisco began in 1974, and the George Washington University museum program started in 1976. Since the early 1980s, a growing number of professional training programs have sprung up around the country, affiliated with art, history, anthropology or science programs in universities.

AAM continually refines the accreditation process. Museum assessment programs and peer review of museums provide important means to assure standards. On a parallel track, professional committees formed to further ongoing education for AAM members. Among other museum disciplines, these committees include small museum administrators, curators and registrars.

The Registrars Committee of the American Association of Museums (RC-AAM), founded in 1977, has produced a myriad of workshops and publications to further best practices and standards for collections stewardship. These include (but are certainly not limited to) work on condition reports, insurance, loan practices and agreements, ethics, couriering, deaccessioning, emergency planning and the development of a standard facility report.

In 1998 more than 70 RC-AAM members contributed to the latest book on museum registration, *The New Museum Registration Methods*, edited by Rebecca A. Buck and Jean Allman Gilmore.

Mechanisms are in place to create and perfect the standards needed to care for museum collections. What is still lacking are standards to deal with problems left from the past, and strong support for wise and careful collecting as well as judicious deaccessioning in museums. In 2004 the American Association of Museums published *Collecting Guidelines for Museums*, which may serve as a template for developing collections and provide the basis for limiting collection problems in the future. The combination of best practices in collections stewardship with an institutional ability to make responsible collection choices can be the foundation for solutions to current problems and prevention of future conundrums.

MUSEUM COLLECTIONS TERMINOLOGY

The Accessioned Object: Definitions and Conundrums

Terms used to describe the status of objects held by a museum mean different things to different people. Museums have remained, for many reasons, decades behind libraries and archives in standardizing the way holdings are acquired, catalogued and deaccessioned. Even the librarians who helped so much to solidify the processing of museum objects—Henry Watson Kent and John Cotton Dana—were unable to impose standards. This is both positive and negative. Differences celebrate the unique character of each museum but also generate confusion whenever it is necessary to communicate or exchange data. Museum workers argue fervently to forward their understandings of a specific term or system. In most cases, the consistent use of terms and systems within an institution is more important than field-wide standards; moving toward standards is, however, laudable.

Shades of definitions exist among different types of museums. Science museum collections are managed differently from art museum collections, for example; thus the procedures and subsequent terminology used to describe the procedures are not completely parallel.[6] The practical gap may be closing, but knowing the history of management and terminology differences remain essential to understanding the collection and its current state. The meanings of terms also change over a long period of time, and it is vital to know the history of a term's use in order to determine what was meant at a specific time. In addition, there are different meanings for terms in the history and culture of individual museums. Institution-specific use must be taken into consideration whenever decisions about collections are made.

Since the meanings of the words color the way in which objects are managed, it is important that everyone understand the history and context of the basic terms. We need only look at the language used in the "Old Loan" laws, the various state property laws or even the variations used by the Smithsonian Institution for found-in-collection (FIC, below) to see that basic terms are not used universally and uniformly. Therefore, to foster communication, promote understanding and forward a standard way of describing the status of museum objects and actions surrounding them, we offer the following discussion of some of the most important terms.

Accession, Accessioned, Accessioning

Accessioning is the two-part process of acquiring an object (acquisition) and documenting an object (registration). The two parts of the process hinge on transfer of title to the museum.

The word most often tossed about without thought of its clear definition is "accession," which, along with its variations, is at the core of collection status. Accession is a noun, a verb and an adjective. The word is not an alternate of acquisition, but is used in conjunction with that word to describe some of the processes and committees museums use when adding objects to their permanent collections.

First, there are published sources that define the term:[7]

- **Accession:** (1) an object acquired by a museum as part of its permanent collection; (2) the act of recording/processing an addition to the permanent collection.
  — Dorothy Dudley and Irma Wilkinson, *Museum Registration Methods*, 3rd ed., 1979

- **Accession:** One or more objects acquired at one time from one source constituting a single transaction between the museum and the source, or the transaction itself.
  — G. Ellis Burcaw, Introduction to *Museum Work*, 3rd ed., 1997

Burcaw goes on to clarify accession by adding a definition for registration: "Assigning a permanent number for identification purposes to an accession and recording this number according to a system." Thus he identifies accessioning, though obliquely, as a process.

In *A Legal Primer on Managing Museum Collections*, Marie Malaro devotes four pages to the meaning of the word "accession." She notes that accessioning is "the formal process used to accept and record an item as a collection object." Everyone dealing with collection status problems should review Malaro's seminal work whenever title questions are being addressed.

The important point is that the word "accessioning" currently includes the process of acquiring, that is, the acquisition of the object as well as its recording. The 1979 edition of *Museum Registration Methods* notes the process only in conjunction with recording, and Burcaw's work does not clarify the process.

Dorothy Dudley was a product of the apprenticeship program at the Newark Museum, class of 1925–26, and the meaning of accessioning at Newark was very clear at the time. Margaret White, registrar there from 1925 through 1940,

wrote an article for *The Museum*, journal of the Newark Museum, called "How a Museum Accessions Objects" in 1925. It indicates that the process started when an object already slated for the permanent collection arrived at the museum. After explaining that John Cotton Dana found a bottle in a Vermont shop in September 1925, which he wanted for the museum's permanent collection, White says:

One morning, soon after, the Museum received the bill and later a box marked "Fragile—Glass." The bottle was unpacked and sent to the Museum registrar. She connected it with the bill, checked the bill and pasted a bit of adhesive tape on the base of the bottle. On the tape she wrote the source, price and date.

Already the gentle art of accessioning . . . has begun.

Dana was a friend of Henry Watson Kent, who developed early "business methods" for the Metropolitan Museum of Art and certainly was aware of Kent's methods. Kent discussed his procedures for acquiring and recording collection objects at the sixth annual AAM meeting in Boston in 1911. The process of accessioning clearly included recording:

At the time of the receipt of the object, the registrar sends to the secretary a card called from its color 'the blue card,' upon which he notes as much information concerning the thing itself as has come under his observation. The return of this card, filled in with additional data furnished by the curator, serves as his notification of the trustees' action. The registrar then accessions the object in a volume which follows in its general arrangement the accession book perfected by librarie. (See sidebar, p. 8)

In current practice the accession process most often includes choice of object, research by curators on origin and provenance, a review of practical considerations, consideration by the personnel and/or committees that the museum has deemed necessary, legal title transfer and warranty, delivery of the object(s) to the museum, assigning and numbering the object(s), developing a base catalogue card and/or computer record and placing the object physically in storage or on exhibition. If we use the verb "accession" to include the entire process of bringing an object into a collection, we are better served when we discuss accessioning in relation to partially accessioned, FIC or supplementary collections.

The noun "accession" is best used to describe the transaction, while the objects involved in the transaction are best represented by the adjective, i.e., accessioned objects. If, as Dudley/Wilkinson used the word, accession denotes an object rather than the transaction, the clear and simple way to track legal status becomes more complicated. If each object is separate, grouping objects with a single source, received at one time, is difficult. The first *Museum Registration Methods* follows through with the "accession as object" definition by assigning either two-part accession numbers or, possibly, three-part numbers if the museum receives a group of objects at the same time.

The definitions we propose to use for accession, then, follow:

- **Accession, verb**: the process used to accept and record an object for the permanent collection of a museum. Acquisition and registration are generally divided by transfer of title.

- **Accession, noun**, as in Burcaw: one or more objects acquired at one time from one source constituting a single transaction between the museum and the source, or the transaction itself.

- **Accessioned or accession, adjective:** describes an object that has been accessioned or something related to the process of accessioning. Examples:

    Accession file
    Accession number
    Accession card
    Accessioned object

Accession Number, Object Number and Catalogue Number

An accession number is a control number, unique to an object, the purpose of which is identification, not description. A catalogue number is a number used to classify or describe an object within a system.

Numbering systems are fascinating, but in the end it is only important that a number used to connect an object to its documentation is unique. That said, there are some very good reasons to use standardized systems.

In the first edition of *Museum Registration Methods*, Dudley and Bezold describe identification numbers in the broad context of their use for accessions, extended loan or loan for exhibition They refer to a type of catalogue number, called "curatorial" number. By the third edition, the glossary compiled by Patricia Nauert was specific in differentiating between the two:

- **Accession number:** a control number, unique to an object, the purpose of which is identification, not description.

- **Catalogue number:** a term used in a variety of ways in museums:

    a. In some museums, a catalogue number is assigned to an object or specimen based on its class; its purpose is description.

    b. In some museums, the number described in this book as an accession number is called a catalogue number, in which case its purpose is identification.

    c. It is the number assigned to an object in a printed publication or catalogue of a special exhibition or collection.

Some museums also refer to object number and differentiate that from the accession number. The accession number in this case, using a tripartite system, includes the first two parts and the object number includes all three.

Acquisition

An "acquisition" is anything acquired by a museum.

All "accessions" are acquired, but not all acquisitions are accessioned. Acquisitions may include everything from real property to office supplies, from exhibit furniture to educational use collections, and may be gifts, transfers, field collections or purchases. Accessions are acquisitions made for the permanent museum collection.

In some museums, the word acquisition describes only objects for permanent collection. In others it may describe additions to study and loan collections, libraries and archives and museum collections. Since it can be used casually to describe anything coming to a museum, it is clearer to avoid the restricted use.

Abandoned Property

"Abandoned Property" is that to which the owner has relinquished all rights.

Care must be taken with the term "abandoned property." Old loans sometimes seem to museum staff—and too often to their lawyers as well—to fall into this area, and some may actually come under a state statute regarding abandoned property. As Malaro notes, however, "For establishing abandonment, the law requires proof of the owner's intention to abandon the property, as well as some affirmative act or omission demonstrating that intention. The burden of proof rests with the party claiming ownership by default." Old loans are usually forgotten property that was not actively tracked and updated by museum staff or by the lender. State law often refers to old loans as "unclaimed" property. Malaro continues: "When an object has been lent to a museum, inferring intention to abandon title when the owner has merely not been heard from for a long time is extremely difficult. Accordingly, the doctrine of abandonment has rarely, if ever, been used effectively in cases of this nature."[8]

If a museum asserts its ownership on the basis of its state's abandoned property law, demonstrating abandonment may result in the property

"escheating" to the state. A remedy that is perfectly adequate for items left in untouched safe-deposit boxes or evacuated apartments is not necessarily good for museum property, which probably has special storage and handling needs that the museum is equipped to provide and historical, artistic or cultural value that dictates its preservation.

It is especially important not to associate the term abandoned property with found-in-collection (FIC) objects or presumed gifts. The law generally sides with the party (the museum) holding the property in claims for ownership, so museums need not actively pursue ownership. If someone claims an object held by a museum without clear title, the evidence of ownership must be clearly and strongly substantiated by the claimant in order for the claim to be granted. Some state legislation dealing with old loans also offers provisions for FIC objects, and decisions regarding the status of all material should be carefully considered before action to clarify title is taken. (See state legislation chart, pp. 28–31) In states without specific remedies in museum-specific legislation, undocumented property could go to a governmental body for eventual sale. FIC objects cannot, by definition as objects with no documentation that have been in the museum for an undetermined amount of time, be identified as abandoned. (See chapter 2 for a more complete discussion of FIC.)

New Jersey law offers a glimpse into the way states may differentiate between abandoned property and the more common forgotten property. New Jersey Statute 46:30C-1 is an act concerning lost or abandoned property. The act defines abandoned property as "property of which the owner has intentionally given up possession under the circumstances evincing intent to give up ownership" and lost property as "property the possession of which has been parted with casually, involuntarily, or unintentionally; or which has been mislaid, left or forgotten."

Though the word pops up occasionally in the sections on treatment of objects, it is best to avoid defining an object as abandoned.

Allocation

"Allocation" is a term used by the federal government of the United States to indicate a restricted transfer of title.

Allocation was a term often used by the Works Progress Administration (WPA) of the federal government to indicate transfer of title to works created during that project. The Operating Procedures in the Public Works of Art Program Bulletin, March 26, 1934, indicates in Section 32, Part A, first paragraph: "For the purposes of this section 'allocated' shall mean transfer of title." However, a later part of the procedure notes a restriction regarding release from the responsibility of custody. The General Services Administration (GSA), in 2000, interpreted the manual to mean that allocated works were transfers of restricted title, and that the "receiving agency or institution received legal title to the works of art limited by the purpose stated in the allocation forms and by the regulations." Art done by WPA programs was often allocated, but it may also have been lent to an institution.

Allocations are most often, in museums, indications of use of funds. If a museum does hold federal project works, however, it is important to become familiar with GSA terms and uses. Carefully check the records of all WPA objects for transfer of title, and seek recourse through with the GSA, which currently oversees WPA works, should there be any question about status.

Catalogue

To "catalogue" is to describe methodically.

It is the level of description and the use of that description that differentiate registrarial cataloguing from curatorial cataloguing. In most museums there is one catalogue for all objects, and registrars provide the first and most physical of descriptions for it: object name, size, medium/material and brief physical description. A photograph is added whenever it is possible. In very large museums, and in particular in science museums, a curatorial catalogue may exist to describe the classification,

history and provenance, medium/material and notes on research. In that case, there should also be a centralized catalogue so that all objects in the museum are represented within the same system. As computerization comes into general use, lines between curatorial and registrarial catalogues—already blurred—are more difficult to discern. It has become ordinary for the most complete and up-to-date catalogue record to be kept in a collections database.

Deposit/On Deposit

The term "deposit" generally means that an object not owned by a museum has been left at the museum for a specific purpose. The purpose may be temporary or long-term loan for exhibition, gift or purchase on approval, study, identification, temporary holding, or any other odd reason for which an object might come to a museum. It does not indicate ownership unless, in the museum's historic use of the term "deposit," it specifically meant "gift," as part of its former operating procedure.

Undocumented Objects and Found in Collection (FIC)

"Undocumented" objects are those objects similar to collections and found-in-collections areas with no numbers, no information in their housing, nor any characteristics that might connect them to documentation. Found-in-collection objects are those undocumented objects that remain after all attempts to reconcile them to existing records of permanent collection and loan objects fail.

"Found-in-collection" or FIC objects are similar to permanent collection objects in type and quality. They have appeared under different names in various museums. FIM, for instance, is the acronym for "found in museum." The Smithsonian Institution archives lists the following subset of terms[9]:

- **Found in Collection**
  Source: National Air and Space Museum, National Museum of American History,

National Museum of the American Indian, National Museum of Natural History

- **Contingency Object**
  Source: National Museum of African Art
  Term used to designate found objects that are unmatched to accession records, but are believed to be accessioned.

- **Museum Acquisition**
  Source: National Museum of American Art

- **Unknown**
  Source: National Museum of the American Indian, National Zoological

- **Unsolicited Gift**
  Source: Cooper-Hewitt Museum

- **X-Number Object**
  Source: National Museum of African Art

The definition of "undocumented objects" is one of the simplest in this group. The peril of the term comes when a museum worker assumes that all undocumented objects belong to the museum, that all are accessioned objects or, on the opposite side, that all are loans, abandoned or forgotten property. Undocumented objects are simply those which cannot be connected to documentation. No status is known.

It is important to track undocumented objects from the moment they are found, although it is not possible to know definitively if they can be reunited with existing documentation until a complete inventory and reconciliation process is done. When a thorough search and examination of records are complete, the remaining undocumented objects are truly found in collection.

Lost Loans

"Lost loans" are those (incoming or outgoing) for which documentation exists but the object cannot be located.

Lost in Inventory

The term "lost in inventory" describes a missing object which has been previously located but is not found when it is needed or during the most current inventory round.

The object may not be truly lost; indeed, it is often moved without a tracking record. Some insurance policies have provisions for property lost in inventory; if an object is not found by repeating the inventory and checking all potential records for loan, removal to conservation, exhibition, etc., it is possible that the object has been stolen. In that case, a claim might be filed with the insurance company.

Loan Collections

"Loan collections" are long-term or extended loans that are used by museums as permanent collections are used.

Loan collections are properly documented by up-to-date loan agreements, renewed annually. Such collections may generally be handled as the museum's permanent collection with regard to storage and exhibition, but any further use, such as lending, publishing or conserving, requires written authorization from the owner.

Old Loans

"Old loans" are objects for which there is documentation (possibly with terms expired) indicating that an owner intended to lend the material; for a loan to be an old loan all contact with the lender must have been lost.

Old loans, as discussed in the section "abandoned property" above, cannot be easily proven to have been abandoned. They are instead usually forgotten objects the ownership of which may well have changed several times through inheritance. Museums never gain ownership of old loans by default, and there are strict limitations on what museums may actively do with loaned material.

Permanent Loan

A "permanent loan" is a long-term loan with no definite termination date.

The term is an oxymoron and should not be used. It does not, in any way, indicate ownership of the objects it covers. Use and disposition must be made within the terms of any existing agreement between the museum and the owner who lent the objects.

Malaro on Permanent Loans

By definition, loans are temporary arrangements, but regardless of what Webster's says, many museums are the possessors of permanent loans. And what is a permanent loan? The definitions are as varied as a roomful of museum professionals ...

In reality, therefore, the term "permanent loan" in itself tells little, and unless the parties spell out in detail precisely what is meant, uncertainty reigns. At best, some permanent loans are in written agreement form describing rights and obligations of the recipient museum. Most are bereft of such instructions, and questions constantly arise.

—Marie Malaro, *A Legal Primer on Managing Museum Collections*, Smithsonian Institution, 1998

Registration

The third edition of *Museum Registration Methods* (MRM) provides a useful definition for "registration" as: "the process of developing and maintaining an immediate, brief, and permanent means of identifying an object for which the institution has permanently or temporarily assumed responsibility." To register an object is to record it according to the registration system in use by the museum.

Temporary Receipt

Museums use several types of receipts to note an object's entrance into or exit from the museum, including shipping receipts, incoming and outgoing receipts, loan receipts, and the more generic "temporary receipt." Temporary receipts were in use before the publication of the first *MRM*, and they covered all material coming into a museum.

The names of receipts, sometimes obvious, sometimes not, should be consistent within an institution; the use of receipts and the procedures that surround them matter more than what they are called. The temporary receipt process often constitutes the first phase of the registration process.

A shipping receipt is usually a simple acknowledgment of shipment and can be issued at the moment of receipt or delivery. This receipt may use the incoming or outgoing receipt form or may differ slightly. It may say "three crates" or "ten dresses" without identifying objects in terms detailed enough to identify each one, although it should note the reason for the object's movement.

A temporary receipt (TR)—or incoming receipt in some museums—is a complex receipt with conditions that specify the terms under which the museum receives an object. It represents the initial registration process. The conditions are much more complex in 2005 than they were in 1958 at the first publication of *MRM*, but the information needed remains essentially the same, with only a few modern technological additions:

- Identifying number as assigned on entry
- Source (name, address, phone, fax, e-mail)
- Date of entry
- Reason for entry into the museum (gift on approval, purchase on approval, exhibition loan, long-term loan, etc.)
- Description of each object
- Disposition note
- Digital photograph on printout of receipt, if possible

Three items of information that were included on the receipt described in the first *MRM* are now usually omitted: value or price, location in museum and record of condition. These three are important parts of the TR file but should not be integral to the actual receipt. Value informa-

The two following blanks should be made out in duplicate and the carbon kept on file:

Loan Receipt No...

NAME OF INSTITUTION

...........19..

Received from............................

as a loan for..............., the objects described

below, subject to the conditions printed on the back

of this sheet.

............Director.

No.	Description of Objects.	Value.

CONDITIONS TO BE PRINTED ON BACK
OF RECEIPT

1. This receipt must in all cases be returned to the Institute upon notification of the action of the Trustees in regard to the objects hereon enumerated.
In the case of accepted loans another receipt will be given, and in the case of purchases or gifts accepted this receipt becomes void.

2. Objects will not be returned to their owners except on presentation and surrender of this receipt, or, if it be lost, upon certification of such fact by the owner, or his legal representative, and presentation of a written order for delivery signed by the owner or by such representative.

3. The Institute will take the same precautions with objects temporarily in its possession as with its own permanent collection, but will not assume any further responsibility for such objects.

If the receipt is not presented when objects are returned a receipt should be given the museum by the person taking the object away.

An early temporary receipt form, from Margaret Talbot Jackson's 1917 publication, *The Museum: A Manual of the Housing and Care of Art Collections.*

tion should remain confidential and consequently should only be noted as necessary in the letter or computer file for the transaction. Complete condition reports should replace a brief record of condition whenever possible. Record of location should be kept within the system the museum uses to record all locations: add a card or computer record for each TR object and update locations as necessary.

The Newark Museum temporary receipt process evolved from the form shown in the first *MRM* and the process of receiving objects now includes:

- Initial cataloguing by the registrar
- Full condition report
- Digital photography
- Entry into collections database
- Tagging with unique number
- Producing micro environments and supports or mounts as necessary
- Placement in storage or exhibition
- Notation of location in the database
- Issuing the TR with complete information (and photograph) to the owner/source

The TR record should also note disposition, i.e., returned, entered into permanent collection, etc., so that there will be a single place to review complete transactions.

Supplemental Collections

Supplemental collections consist of objects useful to museum programs but not meant to be part of the permanent collection.

Various terms are used to describe these collections: reference, study, commodity, university, non-accessioned. In some museums, "supplemental" may describe collections of information about a specific artist or type of collection that goes beyond the items owned or held by that museum.

Collections held by museums, but not part of the permanent collection, must be documented and tracked to avoid confusion with the permanent collection. Some types of supplemental collection are:

- Fakes, forgeries and objects of questionable authorship
- Educational, hands-on collections
- Exhibition props

- Reproductions
- Lending collections
- Study collections

Transaction

"Transaction," as used by museums, describes the entire legal process needed to transfer title or complete a loan.

Unclaimed Property

"Unclaimed property," the term used for old loans in some museum-specific legislation, indicates property lent to or left with another party and not retrieved by the owner.

Unsolicited, Anonymous Gifts

Property known to be left at the museum without documented intent but in a situation where intent can be inferred.

Sometimes referred to as "doorstep donations," each instance of unsolicited gifts must be evaluated to determine if property of unknown origin on museum premises was unintentionally lost or left behind or whether it was purposely left with the intention to make it a gift to the museum.

Notes

1. Marie Malaro, *Legal Primer on Managing Museum Collections* (Washington, DC: Smithsonian Institutions Press, 1998), 4–10.

2. Clarification of terms is vital. See definitions and discussion of the various terms associated with collection status that follows in this chapter.

3. "Object" is used to denote object, artifact, specimen, work of art, etc.

4. Jacquelynn Bass, *Treasures of the Hood Museum of Art* (New York: Hudson Hills Press, 1985), 10.

5. Frederick A. Lucas, "The Evolution of Museums," in *Proceedings of the American Association of Museums [1907 meeting]* (Washington, DC: American Association of Museums, 1908), 82–91

6. This echoes an early AAM presentation that discussed the difficulty science collections faced to keep pace with other types of museums in systematizing their collecting activities.

7. Rebecca Buck and Jean Allman Gilmore, eds., *The New Museum Registration Methods* (Washington, DC: American Association of Museums, 1998), lists both the Dudley/Wilkinson and Burcaw definitions in its glossary.

8. Malaro, *Legal Primer*, 285.

9. http://siarchives.si.edu/collections/tt_acquire.html (accessed Feb. 22, 2007).

2: Conundrums and Their Resolutions

SYSTEMATIC APPROACHES: INTRODUCTION TO OBJECT CONUNDRUMS

The initial recording of objects—if comprehensive and systematic—will help prevent future collection problems, but it will not resolve problems resulting from the lack of such systems in a museum's past. Some common problems include objects found without documentation, loans that are so old that all contact with the lender has been lost, objects with uncertain status, unsolicited deposits and objects that have been partially accessioned. Almost all museums can point to misnumbered objects, objects with duplicate numbers, numbering systems that are too complex or inconsistent numbering systems.

If all old loans and found-in-collection objects can be identified and isolated, if all partially accessioned or misnumbered objects can be flagged, then the museum can deal with the problems with some efficiency. In order to do this, a justified inventory is essential. Inventory, however, has been more honored in the breach than in the reality, as Charles Hummel once wrote.[1]

Inventories may be simple listings of objects found in a particular location. Though of some use, this type of listing has limitations. It tells nothing of the objects that are recorded but not found, nor does it recognize problems in identification. A reconciled inventory, in which each object is carefully checked against its record, gives a complete report of the status of collections. Inventory is the best way to find problems and begin resolution, but it is not always possible to complete thoroughly. Museum workers must develop their own systems, based on the history and tradition of their individual museums, and process collection problems systematically in order to resolve them.

Due diligence, not always achieved in the past, must be pursued in order to resolve collections issues and provide better accountability for collections. A body of procedures to resolve collections problems has accumulated within the profession since the early 1970s. The following chapters lay out the problems and the procedures that can be followed to alleviate them.

The Legal Picture, State by State

In 1979, the term "old loan" did not appear in the glossary of the third edition of *Museum Registration Methods*. At that time one state had a very short and simple law regarding unclaimed loans; the Washington state law, passed in 1975 and applying only to the museum of the University of Washington (Burke Museum), simply noted that unclaimed loans became property of the museum 90 days after actual notification of the lender. There was no indication of what to do should the lender not be found, and nothing in the law that covered undocumented property. This legislation was used only twice, and the Burke Museum now relies on later Washington law that has wider application. The Burke Museum registrar at the time noted that some parties at the university were hesitant to use the authority the law provided.[2]

By 2005, 38 states had passed some form of legislation concerning old loans held by museums. Twenty of these laws covered undocumented property as well as old loans. New York just had a third version of a comprehensive law vetoed and New Jersey museums have launched an attempt to achieve one. Obviously a set of laws governing the disposition and use of objects held by but not owned by museums—and to a lesser degree undocumented property in museums—provides an attractive solution to decades-old problems. These pieces of legislation differ greatly, however, and have not been widely tested in the courts.

Terms for Legislation

Conundrum!

Museums might call them "old loans," but state museum-specific legislation calls them:

- Unclaimed property
- Loaned or undocumented property
- Loans for indefinite or long terms
- Loans to museums
- Property loaned to museums
- Museum property
- Property deposited with museums and historical societies
- Property loaned to museums, archives and libraries
- Abandoned property held by institutions
- Abandoned cultural property

Certain states that undertook such acts managed, at least on their first attempt, to limit the law to only one museum—usually the state museum or perhaps a museum that lobbied for the law without the involvement of a museum organization. The three state historical societies in Washington were surprised and envious to discover that such useful legislation did not apply to them, even as state agencies. Later legislation in Washington, passed in 1988, referred more generally to museums and historical societies. Other states, such as Alabama, still have laws that apply only to specific museums.

Some laws defined museums, some listed libraries or archives in addition to museums and others talked of institutions and defined which institutions might be able to use the law as a remedy. These laws continue to be refined as the problem becomes better understood and need arises.

During the 1990s, the Mid-Atlantic Association of Museums Registrars Committee initiated an Old Loans Task Force that produced a Model Unclaimed Property Act (see appendix A). Led by Jeanne Benas of the National Museum of American History and Jean Gilmore of the Brandywine River Museum, in close consultation with Ildiko DeAngelis, Smithsonian counsel and later director of the George Washington University museum studies program, they reviewed existing loans and property situations in museums within the region and laws in existence across the country. Even though states in the Mid-Atlantic region had no old loan laws at that time and still did not as of 2005, the task force did produce a clear model for legislative language that is not exclusive and not confusing. Arkansas has recently taken advantage of the model.

The model legislation pertains to old loans only, while many state laws cover found-in-collection (FIC) property as well. As discussed later in this chapter, there are substantive differences between FIC and old loans. FIC objects have no documentation; old loans were lent by known persons who can no longer be contacted for known or indefinite periods of time. FIC objects may come from a variety of sources; old loans are loans.

Matchups

Conundrum!

How do museum terms match up with more general terms?

Old Loan	Unclaimed Property
Found in Collection	Undocumented Property
Doorstep Donation	Abandoned Property

Museums in states without old loan legislation may be tempted to rely on the state's abandoned property laws. This course should be taken with advice and caution, since many such laws, which are fashioned to deal with property left in virtually every situation—for example, by renters when they move out of an apartment or by people who never pick up dry cleaning—often stipulate that the property or proceeds from the property revert to the state. Assuming an old loan to be abandoned is also dangerous. It is not impossible for a museum to receive a claim for a loan that is 50 or 60 years old. If an old loan problem exists, the best course of action is to work with state agencies dedicated to the arts, other museums and museum associations and sympathetic legislators to pass appropriate legislation.

Policies and procedures to manage old loans differ from those for FIC objects. Since old loans will never belong to the museum unless action is taken, the policy can be simple and the procedures clear. Not acting does nothing positive for the museum. Policy might include a statement acknowledging that old loans may exist in the collection and that the museum will take action in accordance with the laws of the state in which the museum sits to gain title to such materials.

Policy and procedures for FIC material are complex and entail difficult decisions. A museum may follow an assertive track to claim the property, or it may more quietly claim that the property belongs to the museum and handle it accordingly.

In the opinion of DeAngelis, a museum's best course is to treat FIC material as if it were museum property and to make a positive statement of ownership. That statement could be formal accessioning, exhibition, publication, actual notice or constructive notice—all actions that strengthen the ownership position of the museum. Should a claim be made, the law generally sides with the museum; the burden to prove ownership falls on the claimant. Proof of sole ownership or an explicit agreement to act for all owners is difficult to produce and becomes more so as the length of time an object is held unclaimed by a museum increases.

In 1983 Judith L. Teichman argued for the support of a California law for museums and suggested that the law might cover objects of uncertain status as well as objects on loan.[3] She concludes her paper on support of California legislation with this statement: "The solution to the problems of unclaimed and unidentified objects in the possession of museums must apply uniformly, and the result of its application in specific cases must be clear . . . . Legislation which is precisely tailored to the factors which create the problem is the approach most likely to achieve the desired end." The eventual California law covered only old loans, not undocumented or FIC property. Teichman, in a later article, reaffirmed her belief that legislation for resolution of undocumented property in museums is needed: "On a prospective and constructive note, several states have adopted legislation dealing with abandoned property in museums, and more states need, and are considering, such legislation."[4]

Michigan's law, passed in 1992, included provisions for undocumented property, defined as "property in the possession of a museum, the owner or lender of which the museum has no reasonable means of identifying." The law indicates that a museum does not gain title to undocumented property that has been in its possession for 35 years or more unless specific notification and time guidelines are met. According to Pam Watson of the Detroit Institute of Arts, the cost of publication in the type and size required prevents the museum from pursuing ownership for all items in question by using this law.

Museums often seek legislative solutions to collection ambiguities because property cannot be freely used or disposed of unless the museum has ownership. Such a solution is imperative for old loans because they never revert to the museum. It is not as urgent for undocumented property, since it is likely the museum already owns that property. In fact, undocumented property legislation can increase a museum's risk if it is not followed and can put the museum in jeopardy of negative publicity, spurious claims and excessive cost if it is. In Michigan the law specifically notes that property cannot be claimed by the museum unless all of the provisions of the act are followed, so museums there have no choice but to follow the law to the letter if they wish to dispose of property.

If a state's old loan legislation covers objects without documentation, that law in general supersedes any other state property laws that might exist. In some states, such as California, the common property law still applies in specific cases.

Museum workers should consider all aspects of the problem of undocumented property before proceeding to a remedy as outlined in the law. The first part of the process, finding undocumented material in the museum whether through inventory or through day-to-day work on projects such as exhibitions, loans and rehousing, is constrained mostly by time and staff limitations. Once the material is found, staff can begin reconciliation, a process that can take decades or may not be attempted at all. Reconciliation involves determining whether anything in the group of undocumented objects matches documents on file. When reconciliation is complete, decisions must be made regarding the remaining group of undocumented objects. The museum may choose to simply treat the objects as if they were its own or to follow the laws of the state, either museum-specific or common, in making a formal ownership declaration. Museum administrators and trustees must consider all risks and understand the consequences of whatever course of action they decide to take.

Each museum must debate the options carefully and may reach the conclusion that the resulting policy should reflect different decisions for different classes of material. It may not, for example, be worth staff time to follow the law assertively, going through the process of constructive notice and enduring a long waiting period in order to dispose of undocumented silk garments from the 1920s that are in tatters because of inherent vice. If the property is of little value, the chance of a potential claim is almost nonexistent. The operative phrase in this situation is *de minimis*, "a legal term for an amount that is small enough to be ignored, too small to be taken seriously."[5]

On the other hand, a series of original drawings, made by a known though perhaps not renowned artist, may be worth all the time and effort it takes to claim them. The important consideration in every case is how much risk the museum is willing to take. The deaccession risk chart on page 48 can help determine this. The primary factors (low versus high risk) include: multiples versus originals, little or no monetary value versus high monetary value, very bad versus excellent condition, gift to another institution versus destruction or sale and full documentation versus no documentation.

Museum workers must be aware of all state laws regarding property; they should consult with legal counsel for general guidance and specific advice and they should make their policy decisions with involvement of their trustees.

Lobbying

Conundrum!

Should you lobby for legislation to gain title to undocumented property?

It is prudent, when working with a state legislature to pass museum-specific legislation, to collaborate with professional groups and large museums within the state and to debate this issue carefully. In New Jersey, for example, the groups supporting legislation are the New Jersey Association of Museums, the Advocates for New Jersey History and the Newark Museum. Look at the legislation that has passed to see if it is cumbersome, clear and worthwhile. Remember that the law will affect all museums in the state and try not to include provisions that will prove burdensome or unduly restrictive to the smallest historical museum or the largest art or natural history museum. Make informed decisions.

Notes on Museum Property Laws by State

It is not possible to guarantee that the information in this section is complete or up-to-date. It is provided as a guideline only, and museums should always begin collection reconciliation and return projects by contacting an attorney who is familiar with state law.

Laws are introduced, amended and repealed continuously. Check for updates or changes before work pertaining specifically to the laws listed below begins. Most of these laws can readily be found on the Internet by searching for state laws and then accessing the designated chapters.

Almost all of the laws require a museum to inform interested parties of its intention to claim ownership of property in its possession—both old loans and undocumented property—and when it is covered, by giving actual notice: that is, a certified letter with specific language sent directly to the last known address of the owner. If direct notice does not result in contact with the owner, then the museum must give constructive notice, usually in the form of a public notice run for a specified period of time in a newspaper in the area where the museum sits and/or in the county of the last known address of the owner. Either type of notice must be followed by a prescribed waiting period. After the waiting period runs out, the loaned objects become property of the museum.

Due diligence may require a museum to do much more to find an owner than send a notice to the last known address on file or publish notice in a newspaper. It is important to spend some time looking for lost lenders, donors and artists. Conducting such a search strengthens the museum's position in assuming ownership.

As of 2005, 18 states have museum-specific legislation pertaining only to old loans, 20 have legislation covering both old loans and FIC and 12 have no museum-specific legislation. New York State, which has legislation only for the state museum, has tried and failed three times to have general legislation passed and signed. In addition, the District of Columbia has no legislation specific to museums.

Legislation chart

Summary			
	States with loans only	18	
	States with loans/FIC	20	
	No state laws	13 (with DC)	
State	Citation	Comments	FIC
Alabama	§ 41-6-70 to 41-6-75	Applies only to collections held by the Department of Archives and History.	No
Alaska	§ 14.57.200 to 14.57.290	Article 1 applies to the State Museum. Article 3 applies to property held by museums; notifications of all Native American FIC property must be sent to all Native Corporations.	"Undocumented Property" must be held for 7 years or longer, verified by museum records, with no contact or claim by any person. The museum must publish a notice once a week for 4 weeks including specified information. If the property is not Native American, the museum can claim title on the 46th day after the last notice.
Arizona	§ 44-351 to 44-356		"Undocumented Property" must be held for 7 years or longer, verified by museum records, with no contact or claim by any person. The museum must: publish a notice for 2 consecutive weeks including specified information, wait 65 days, then publish a second notice including specified information. If no claims are made, title passes to the museum.

Arkansas	§ 13-5-1001 to 13-5-1013		"Undocumented Property" that is documented by the museum for 7 years, to which no person has made a claim, becomes the property of the museum. However, ownership is NOT vested if the undocumented property is determined later to be stolen property or property whose ownership is subject to federal law.
California	§ 1899 to 1899.11		No
Colorado	§ 38-14-101 to 38-14-112		No
Connecticut		No museum-specific legislation, as of 2005	
Delaware		No museum-specific legislation, as of 2005.	
District of Columbia		No museum-specific legislation, as of 2005.	
Florida	§ 265.565.1-12		No
Georgia		No museum-specific legislation, as of 2005.	
Hawaii		No museum-specific legislation, as of 2005.	
Idaho		No museum-specific legislation, as of 2005.	
Illinois	chap. 765 § 1033/1 to 1033/50	For FIC, no notice is necessary. The only requirement is for the 7 year waiting period to end.	"Undocumented Property" that is held by the museum for 7 years, to which no person has made a claim, becomes the property of the museum. However, ownership is NOT vested if the undocumented property is determined later to be stolen property or property whose ownership is subject to federal law.
Indiana	§ 32-9-10-1 to 32-9-10-16		"Undocumented Property" must be held for 7 years or longer. The museum must publish a notice including specified information. If no claims are made within 3 years of the publication of the notice, title passes to the museum.
Iowa	§ 305B.1 to 305B.13		"Undocumented Property" must be held for 7 years or longer, with no contact or claim by any person. The museum must publish a notice including specified information. If no claims are made within 3 years of the publication of the notice, title passes to the museum.
Kansas	§ 58-4001 to 58-4013		"Undocumented Property" must be held for 7 years or longer, with no contact or claim by any person. The museum must publish a notice including specified information. If no claims are made within 1 year of the publication of the notice, title passes to the museum.
Kentucky	§ 171.830 to 171.849		No
Louisiana	§ 25.345	Applies only to Louisiana State museums.	Any property that is held at a museum for 10 years or more, to which no person has made a claim, becomes the property of the museum if the museum publishes a notice once a week for 2 weeks containing specified information. If no claims are made within 65 days, title passes to the museum.
Maine	tit. 27, § 601		Any property that is held at a museum for 25 years or more, to which no person has made a claim, becomes the property of the museum if the museum publishes a notice once a week for 2 weeks containing specified information. If no claims are made within 65 days, title passes to the museum.
Maryland		No museum-specific legislation, as of 2005.	

Massachusetts		No museum-specific legislation, as of 2005.	
Michigan	§ 399.601 to 399.612		Beginning January 1, 1993, a museum may give notice on "Undocumented Property." The museum must publish a notice for 2 consecutive weeks including specified information, wait at least 60 days, then publish a second notice including specified information.
Minnesota	345.70 to 345.74		No
Mississippi	§ 39-19-1 to 39-19-21		No
Missouri	§ 184.101 to 184.122		"Undocumented Property" must be held for 7 years or longer, with no contact or claim by any person. The museum must publish a notice including specified information. If no claims are made within ninety days of the publication of the notice, title passes to the museum.
Montana	§ 22-3-501 to 22-3-523		No
Nebraska	§ 51-701 to 51-712		"Undocumented Property" must be held for 7 years or longer, with no contact or claim by any person. The museum must publish a notice including specified information. If no claims are made within three years of the publication of the notice, title passes to the museum.
Nevada	§ 381.009	Applies only to certain Nevada State museums and historical societies.	Any property that is held at a museum for 3 years or more, to which no person has made a claim, becomes the property of the museum if the museum publishes a notice once a week for 2 weeks containing specified information. If no claims are made within 60 days, title passes to the museum.
New Hampshire	§ 201-E:1 to 201-E:7		"Undocumented Property" must be held for 5 years or longer, with no contact or claim by any person. The museum must publish a notice including specified information. If no claims are made within 90 days of the publication of the notice, title passes to the museum.
New Jersey		No museum-specific legislation, as of 2005.	
New Mexico	§ 18-10-1 to 18-10-5		No
New York	§ 233-a	Applies only to the New York State museum. More general legislation that would have applied to all museums in the state was vetoed twice by the governor. As of late 2005, no such law is in place.	"Undocumented Property" must be held for 5 years or longer, with no contact or claim by any person. The museum must publish a notice including specified information. If no claims are made within 180 days of the publication of the notice, title passes to the museum.
North Carolina	§ 121-7(c) and 121-7(d)	Applies only to North Carolina State museums.	"Undocumented Property" must be held for 5 years or longer, with no contact or claim by any person. The museum must publish a notice including specified information. If no claims are made within 30 days of the publication of the notice, title passes to the museum.
North Dakota	§ 47-07-14	Personal/Movable Property General Provision	No
Ohio	tit. 33 § 3385.01 -.10		No
Oklahoma*	60.683.2*		No
Oregon	§ 358.415 to 358.440		No
Pennsylvania		No museum-specific legislation, as of 2005.	
Rhode Island		No museum-specific legislation, as of 2005.	
South Carolina	§ 27-45-10 to 27-45-100		No

South Dakota	§ 43-41C-1 to 43-41C-4		Abandoned Property: Any property that has been held by the museum for 10 years or more, other than by terms of a loan agreement, shall be deemed abandoned. The museum must publish a notice with specific information. If no claims are made within 65 days, title passes to the museum.
Tennessee	§ 66-29-201 to 66-29-204		Abandoned Property: Any property that has been held by the museum for 20 years or more, other than by terms of a loan agreement, shall be deemed abandoned. The museum must publish a notice with specific information. If no claims are made within 65 days, title passes to the museum.
Texas	§ 80.001 to 80.008		No
Utah	§ 9-8-801 to 9-8-806		Any materials that are not accompanied by a transfer of title are considered a gift when more than 25 years have passed from the date of the last written contact between depositor or his successors and the collecting institution.
Vermont		No museum-specific legislation, as of 2005.	
Virginia	§ 55-210.31 to § 55-210.38		No
Washington	§ 63.26.010 to 63.26.050		Abandoned Property: Any property that has been held by the museum for 5 years or more, other than by terms of a loan agreement, shall be deemed abandoned. The museum must publish a notice with specific information at least once a week for 2 weeks. If no claims are made within 90 days, title passes to the museum.
West Virginia		No museum-specific legislation, as of 2005.	
Wisconsin	§ 171.30 to 171.33		No
Wyoming	§ 34-23-101 to 34-23-108		No

*Pursuant to section 60.683.2(c) of the Oklahoma statutes, a museum is exempted from the provisions of the state's Uniform Unclaimed Property Act, but may avail itself to the provisions of the act by complying with its provisions. It is not certain whether the Oklahoma legislature intended a museum's use of the provisions under the act to resolve old loan problems.

—Courtesy of Kathryn Speckart, Collections Manager, United States Diplomacy Center
Assistance provided by Sarah Heffron, Graduate Assistant, Museum Studies Program, George Washington University

OLD LOANS

Ildiko DeAngelis

Very few museum registrars are spared the vexing problem of "old loans." The term refers to expired loans or loans of unlimited duration left unclaimed by lenders who cannot be readily located by the museum.[6] These objects may have come to the museum under formal loans for exhibition purposes or under temporary custody arrangements for examination or study by museum staff.[7] The lenders have long since died, moved or, in any case, have failed to maintain contact with the museum. As registrars are routinely assigned responsibility to monitor loans and to account for objects and their documentation in the custody of the museum, it is to this office that the task of resolving the old loan conundrum is usually assigned.

History!

Newly organized small museums are inclined to accept gratefully interesting materials as indefinite loans from local citizens in order to improve the appearance of their recently arranged exhibit cases. Quite a number of small history museums have in their collections articles accepted at various times in the past as long-term loans. This means that these museums are responsible for property that does not belong to them. This is bad business practice. The leaders among museums urge strongly that small museums scrupulously avoid this practice as a means of enhancing a museum's collections.

—Carl E. Guthe, *The Management of Small History Museums*, AASLH, 1959

Because day-to-day tasks quickly consume a registrar's time, often little or none remains to spare on old loans.[8] Nevertheless, museums and registrars are well advised to make time for old loans because the mere passage of time will not cure the problem and often the older the loan

gets, the harder it may be to resolve. Lacking legal title to the unclaimed objects, the museum can make only limited use of them, all the while bearing the costs and burdens of storage space, record maintenance, climate control, security, periodic inspection, insurance and general overhead.[9]

To understand what must be done, it is important to appreciate the legal constraints involved. The basic legal relationship between the lender and the museum is a "bailment," under which the museum as "bailee" (borrower) generally has the obligation to care for the object until the "bailor" (lender) reclaims it.[10] This obligation can go on indefinitely because the passage of time will not alter this legal relationship. For example, if a lender dies, his or her ownership interest in the object will pass to heirs. Often, determining the identity and location of heirs entitled to the object may be a difficult and time consuming if not an impossible task. To make things worse, returning the object to the wrong party may open the museum to liability for a claim brought by the rightful owner.

The key to resolving the old loan dilemma is for the museum to break the bailment relationship as soon as possible. Unfortunately, this is not easily done under general legal principles.

In recognition of these difficulties, 38 states, as of 2005, have passed old loan statutes that specifically make this task easier for museums.[11] These old loan laws spell out the mechanisms by which the lender's ownership of the object can be cut off, making it possible for the museum to move with some assurance toward gaining title to the object. With the title secure, the museum then may use or dispose of an object as it sees fit. More will be said about these state statutes and the general approaches they take but first, a discussion of "common law" principles (principles that govern in absence of a statute) is in order. These principles usually prevail in states without specific old loan statutes, and knowledge of these principles also assists in appreciating and/or interpreting specific old loan statutes.

1. The Common Law Solution

In states without old loan statutes, museums depend on general principles of common law to guide them. Common law refers to principles that do not rest their authority on any express statute, but upon statements of principles found in court decisions. The application of these principles to old loans has not been fully tested in court. As a result, museums are left with some legal uncertainties.[12] Nevertheless, under these principles, to break the bailment relationship, the museum must take actions inconsistent with the terms of the bailment and call the lender's attention to the fact that title to the object is being challenged and could be lost if the lender remains silent. For example, the museum should send a letter to the lender stating that the museum is terminating the loan and unless the lender comes forward to claim the objects or make arrangements for their successful return by a certain date, the museum will take title to the objects as of that date. If the lender is aware of the museum's "conversion" (a legal term meaning unauthorized assumption of ownership of property belonging to another), the lender, under general principles of law, must come forward to protect his or her ownership interests. If the lender fails to claim the object or to bring his or her claim or suit to court within a specific time after the museum's conversion of the object, the lender's ownership rights may be lost because of what we call "statutes of limitations."

The specific time periods to bring claims to court are provided in state laws, called statutes of limitations. Lawsuits are barred that are not brought within prescribed limitation periods. The purpose of statutes of limitations is to encourage claimants to take timely action before evidence fades and witnesses die. Statutes of limitations vary from state to state and with the nature of the claim. For example, a claim for breach of contract will have a different limitation period from a claim based on negligence causing personal injury. Although it is relatively simple to determine the length of the limitation period in any state for a claim of "conversion," the more difficult issue is to determine when the limitation period against an owner to extinguish his claim begins. The general rule is that the owner of property "converted" by another must bring his or her claim to court within the limitation period that begins after his or her "cause of action" arises. A "cause of action" is a set of facts that give a person the right to file a suit in court.

Under the law of bailment, the "cause of action" usually arises when the lender demands return of the object and the borrower refuses. The lender's cause of action may also arise when he or she is put on notifice that the borrower is claiming title to the object, in effect, refusing to return the object. Thus, to utilize the statute of limitations to extinguish a lender's right to an unclaimed object, the museum must make sure the lender has been notified that the museum intends to terminate the loan and claim the loaned object as its own if the lender fails to reclaim it or arrange for its return.[13]

To ensure that the limitations period is triggered, the museum should notify the lender by certified mail, return receipt requested, to prove that the lender received actual notice of the museum's actions. The limitations period begins upon receipt of the notice, and after its expiration, the lender who has failed to take action should be barred from any further claim to the object. Title to the object, in effect, then belongs to the museum. At this time, the museum is free to do whatever it wishes with the object—keep it, lend it or dispose of it.

History!

Lenders can become administrative nuisances. They or their heirs may object to the ways in which their loans are used and cared for. A sensible procedure is to take immediate steps to transform any existing long-term loans into gifts, or to arrange their return to their owners or their heirs.

—Carl E. Guthe, *The Management of Small History Museums*, AASLH, 1959

Anyone who has ever worked with old loans inevitably asks the next question: What if the lender is unknown or the lender or heirs cannot be located? Are there any alternatives to actual notice? One court decision from the District of Columbia, in the McCagg case, involved an old loan, and the court suggested that "constructive notice" to the lender might be legally sufficient where actual notice is not possible. The term "constructive notice" refers to notice to unknown or missing individuals by publication in a newspaper. If done properly, the law will presume that the notice reached the individual whether or not he or she actually saw the notice in the newspaper. All the old loan statutes discussed below have implemented the "constructive notice" approach to notify missing lenders. The question remains whether "constructive notice" will be legally sufficient without an applicable state statute in place that provides how and when this may be done. Until this has been tested in court, museums must face an element of uncertainty in this area. This uncertainty should not prevent museums from proceeding, because doing nothing affords no chance of yielding any positive results. Each museum is urged, however, to consult with its legal counsel before initiating notice to lenders by publication.

In any event, the court in the McCagg case cautioned that constructive notice may be available only if actual notice is not possible. Thus, a museum must be in a position to show that after reasonable efforts the lender or heirs could not be located. As to what constitutes reasonable efforts, once again there is little guidance in existing legal precedent. One commentator suggests that museums should consult their own records in addition to the following sources: probate records, telephone directories, real estate records and vital (death) records.[14] Depending on the circumstances, other avenues such as social registers or cemetery records may be available. In this Internet age, it may be much easier to locate a missing lender using web-based resources. The utility of the Internet to assist museum staff with such searches is improving yearly as more information becomes available online, such as estate records and newspapers' archives of obituaries.[15] It is absolutely essential that the museum document every effort taken to locate lenders because the museum's records may become evidence should a lender or heir suddenly surface years later and demand return of the object. The value of the objects in question may have an impact on the extent of efforts to locate the lenders. If, after reasonable efforts, the whereabouts of the lender or heirs are still unknown, the museum may publish "constructive notice" in a newspaper.

The notice in the newspapers should include as much of the following information as possible:

- Date of the notice

- Name of the lender

- Description of the item loaned

- Date of the original loan

- Name and address of the museum staff to contact

- Statement that the museum is terminating the loan and will take title to the object if it is not claimed by a specified date

It is suggested that this notice should be published once a week for three consecutive weeks in a newspaper of general circulation in the county of the lender's last known address and the county or municipality where the museum is located.[16] The statute of limitations should begin to run after the date set in the notice as a deadline for contacting the museum—whether or not the lender or heirs have actually seen the published notice.

If the lender fails to come forward before the date given by actual or constructive notice, the museum should amend its records immediately to reflect the ownership change for the object as of that date. In addition, the museum should note in the records the date of expiration of claims under that state's statute of limitations. Although the museum asserts ownership from the date the object is accessioned, its title to the object is subject to challenge in a claim brought to court by the lender or heirs up to the time the applicable limitations period for filing suit has expired. Therefore, the file should note that prior to the expiration of the statute of limitations, the object should not be disposed of by the museum. For example, a museum publishes notice that the date in which title is claimed will be June 1, 2007. Having failed to hear from the lender or heirs, on June 1, 2007, the museum accessions the object. Having been advised by counsel that the limitations period for "conversion" is three years in the state where the museum is located, the museum will note in the records that the object should not be disposed of prior to June 2, 2010.

In planning a systematic approach to resolve old loans in states where no statute exists, museums are well advised to seek the advice of counsel in establishing procedures and forms for this purpose. One highly recommended publication to aid museums and their counsel in this effort is entitled "Practical Guidelines in Resolving Old Loans: Guidelines for Museums" by Agnès Tabah.[17] This paper has step-by-step instructions and sample forms that may be very helpful.

However, because of a lack of clear precedents, even if all recommended steps are taken, there are no guarantees that claims will not be brought against the museum for "conversion" of the loaned object. In the worst case, a lender or heirs may surface years later and institute a lawsuit. At this point, if a court should determine that the steps taken by the museum to gain title were legally insufficient, the museum may be required to return the object. If the object was disposed of in the interim, the museum may be ordered to compensate the lender for the value of the object, possibly as of the date of the lender's reappearance. Although the risk of a legal suit with the attendant adverse publicity should not be underestimated, this risk needs to be balanced against the substantial benefits gained by freeing the museum's collections from unwanted objects that are costly to maintain, and by having reliable, up-to-date records of objects in its collections. If

the objects are of little value, it is unlikely that anyone is ever going to sue. If someone does threaten a lawsuit, it is a relatively simple matter to offer to pay him or her the value of the object to resolve the claim. If the museum has disposed of the object after acquiring title, it should have an excellent record of the object's value at the time of disposal. In any event, the museum's counsel may be able to negotiate a settlement without a formal legal proceeding.

2. Legislative Solution: State Old Loan Statutes

A list of states that have passed old loan statutes appears elsewhere in this book (see legislation chart, pp. 28–31). For a museum located in one of these states, resolving old loans will require following the dictates of the applicable statute. While state old loan statutes vary in approach, they all establish specific mechanisms by which the museum may terminate the loan and take title to objects left unclaimed by lenders. In operation, the legislative solution mimics the common law approach but adds clarity and some degree of certainty of the adequacy of the procedures. In some cases, old loan statutes eliminate some cumbersome steps required under the common law approach. The usual scheme is for the law to prescribe a notice procedure by which lenders are notified by the museum that the loan is terminated. The notice procedures may apply to expired loans as well as to indefinite loans that have been at the museum for an extended period.

The notice may take two general forms. The first is by mail to the lender of record at his or her last known address. The second is notice by publication in newspapers. Some statutes only require notice by mail to the name and address of the lender as it appears in the museum's records. If that information is not accurate or if it is incomplete, no further search for the lender is required. Other statutes require a "reasonable search" for the lender, often not giving much guidance as to what the term means. If the lender cannot be reached by mail, the museum may proceed with notification by publication in a newspaper. If, after notice, no one comes forward to make a claim within the prescribed time period (ranging from 30 days to 7 years), title to the object passes to the museum. Several states allow museums to take title to an object without giving notice if there was no contact between the museum and the lender for a long time. For example, California allows the museum to take title if there has been no contact with the lender for at least 25 years as evidenced in the museum's records.[18]

In addition, old loan statutes may impose obligations on lenders to notify museums of change of address and changes in ownership of the property.[19] Some statutes address the issue of undertaking conservation work on unclaimed loans.[20]

An important question not yet answered is whether these statutes will pass constitutional challenges that may be brought to court by disgruntled lenders. Such challenges to state laws may be brought under the 14th Amendment of the U.S. Constitution, alleging that the old loan statute deprives the lender of his or her property without the "due process of law." The question presented in such cases is whether the law affords owners adequate notice and opportunity to protect their ownership rights before such rights are cut off. As of 1997, there have been no published court decisions testing the constitutionality of any state old loan statute, and we have yet to see how a court may view these statutes with regard to due process questions.

An unpublished study from about 15 years ago indicates that many museums at that time were not fully utilizing applicable old loan statutes. This conclusion was based on sparse replies to a questionnaire on implementation of old loan legislation.[21] The study posits the following reasons for this sluggishness. To use the statutes systematically, museums need to inventory their collections to determine which objects are in fact old loans. Inventories require time and effort and are too easily relegated to low priority. Also, some

museums may be reluctant to implement the statutes, fearing that important objects will be lost if lenders actually come forward and reclaim loaned objects. Finally, some may fear the administrative burdens that may be presented by spurious claims. The experience reported by the few museums who have implemented their legislation, however, shows the opposite.

Contrary to fears, large numbers of people did not come forward to claim objects. Moreover, implementation of the old loan statutes gave registrars a useful instrument to provide vacillating lenders incentive to make decisions on disposition of their loaned property.[22]

3. How to Avoid the Problem of Old Loans in the Future

Given the time, effort and costs involved in resolving old loans, museums should institute safeguards to avoid this problem in the future. Museums should borrow objects for a limited duration only (usually one year) with the expiration date specifically stated in the loan agreement. If the object is needed longer, it is better to renew the loan than to agree to a longer initial term. More frequent contact with lenders will avoid the missing lender situation. Loan agreements should specify that it is the lender's obligation to notify the museum of a change in the lender's address or a change in the ownership of the loaned object. Moreover, loan agreements should state that if, at the expiration of the loan, the museum is unable to contact the lender to make arrangements for the return of the object, the museum will store the object for a set period of years at the lender's expense. If, after this period, the lender still fails to come forward after notice by mail is sent by the museum to the lender's address of record, the museum will deem that an unrestricted gift of the object is made by the lender to the museum. In effect, the loan agreement will put the lender on notice of the museum's claim to the object after a set period of time if the lender fails to maintain contact or refuses to pick up the object.

Objects left at the museum for identification, authentication or examination are more likely to be left unclaimed than objects borrowed by the museum for exhibition purposes. The negligible value of some of these objects may remove an incentive for their owners to return to claim them. To avoid this risk, these objects should be processed immediately by the museum. Each should be documented with a temporary custody receipt, signed by the owner. If an object was mailed unsolicited to the museum, the package should be returned within days to the sender. If more time is needed, the temporary custody receipt should be mailed to the sender for signature. The length of the museum's custody specified in the receipt should be limited to a period significantly shorter than the duration of a standard incoming loan. For example, a museum may decide that the maximum time for temporary custody is three months, subject to extension by special permission only. The temporary custody receipt should specify the exact method to be used for return of the object and include a provision, similar to one used in a formal loan agreement, that infers a gift to the museum if the object is not claimed after a limited storage period subsequent to the expiration date on the receipt.

Conclusion

As a public trust, a museum has a legal responsibility to make the best use of its assets. Prudent collections management dictates that museums should pursue systematic efforts to clean up old loans that occupy valuable storage space and consume scarce staff and financial resources. But procedures should also be in place to avoid these situations. It is the registrar's office that usually plays a critical role in developing and implementing ways to banish the old loan problem in a museum.

Conundrum!

Should an extended or long-term loan be registered in the same way as an object in the permanent collection?

Documentation should be similarly extensive for a loan or a permanent collection object, but a different series of numbers should be used. For instance, if your museum is using 2007.3.1 for the first object in the third accession in 2007, the first object in the third loan could be dubbed L2007.3.1 or L3.2007.1. Since the third edition of *Museum Registration Methods* states: "In terms of record keeping, extended loans are often treated as part of the permanent collection," it is wise to look closely at all collection documentation to determine if any loans are lurking among the gifts and purchases in the permanent collection.[23]

FOUND IN COLLECTION

Overview

Almost all museum collections contain some objects that have no number, no tag, no indication of source in their packaging and no characteristic that connects them to records of gifts, purchases, loans or other documentation. They are found during inventories, they are discovered during work on an exhibition or a rehousing project or they pop up when someone leaves the institution and their desks and shelves are cleaned out.

These objects may have entered the collection at any time in the museum's history. They may have been gifts, purchases, bequests or objects left in spaces taken over by the museum; they may have been loans or objects left from special events or educational programs. They may have been objects belonging to former staff, brought in for decoration; they may even have been former utilitarian objects that, by their age and manufacture, have attained some historical or aesthetic value. Even though their status may be uncertain, it is more likely than not that they belong to the museum.

Sources

Conundrum!

What are the sources for undocumented objects?

- Gift
- Gift on approval/deposit
- Bequest
- Bequest on approval/deposit
- Field collecting
- Purchase
- Purchase on approval/deposit
- Commission
- Unclaimed or "old loan"
- Abandoned property
- Exhibition prop
- Special events prop
- Made on site
- Educational programs
- Arts workshop
- Exhibition workshop
- Acquired with real property
- Decoration
- Former office/storage equipment
- Staff personal property
- Awards and trophies (museum or staff)

Undocumented objects are mysteries, but many times the mystery can be solved. If it is solved, the undocumented object returns to its true status as a loan, gift or purchase. If it cannot be solved, then the object may properly be considered a found-in-collection (FIC) object. In order to protect the museum's interests, should claims regarding these objects arise, it is necessary to differentiate between the two status types.

The museum profession has not unanimously decided on terminology for this collection problem and discussion about these objects is often confusing. It is important that the museum community come to a more uniform understanding of the definitions used to discuss the problem. The two important terms, with the definitions we propose, are "undocumented object" and "found in collection" (FIC).

- **Undocumented objects** are those objects similar to collections and found-in-collections areas with no numbers, no information in their housing nor any characteristics that might connect them to documentation.

- **Found-in-collection** objects are undocumented objects that remain without status after all attempts to reconcile them to existing records of permanent collection and loan objects fail. In other words, undocumented objects become FIC after sufficient research fails to identify them.

It is vital to track undocumented objects from the moment they are found, but is not possible to know definitively if they can be connected to existing documentation until a complete inventory and reconciliation process is done. When it is, the remaining objects can be called found in collection and may be considered museum property.

Many factors influence the type and quantity of objects that are undocumented. If a museum collects objects or works of art with a fairly narrow focus, if almost all objects are of high value, if the museum is fairly young and/or if the collection has historically been tightly controlled, then the chances of having FIC material is slight. New museums, and many established art museums, either do not have FIC or have a very minor occurrence of this type of object. Unfortunately, these museums are few and FIC objects are common across the museum field. The problem is widespread, not attributable to one cause and certainly not anything that should incur blame on current staff. Most FICs are the product of the lack of caretakers for the collections and the vagaries of past collecting practices.

Bad practices

Conundrum!

What types of practices lead to undocumented objects?

- Documentation systems were not regularized for museums until the early 1900s. The dissemination of those systems was slow, and staff to implement them scarce.

- Different systems were embraced—and reinvented—by different museums. Several systems for accessioning and documenting objects often exist within one museum.

- Natural history, history, anthropology and archaeology museums work with such large volumes of material that adequate staffing is rarely an option. Some objects just never got processed.

- Volunteers have been used extensively for collections work, and they are not always well trained or clearly committed to finishing tasks at hand. Supervision and checking of work are not always possible because of the volume of work and the lack of professional staff.

- The entire tenor of society in the first part of the 20th century, when museums were forming, was very informal with regard to property transfer. The litigious nature of the early 21st century was virtually unknown.

- Tax laws have, especially since the middle of the 20th century, pushed recording of gifts in a timely fashion to the forefront of collection activities. Before there were IRS incentives or IRS reporting, timelines for gifts were much more casual.

- Human nature is probably the largest cause. Directors and curators took in unimportant objects from important donors rather than upset them. Board members felt that the museums were an extension of their own collections and deposited, donated and purchased accordingly.

Policy

There are divergent opinions about undocumented and FIC objects and how they should be treated by a museum. The first and perhaps most difficult task is to find all undocumented objects and to reconcile as many of them as possible to existing documentation. At the end of the inventory process a museum is usually left with a number of objects that are lost in inventory and a number of objects that are undocumented. The reconciliation process has, in the past, been hit or miss, protracted and difficult. Searching through a card catalogue system or inventory books, however well developed, can be like searching for a needle in a haystack. The advent of computerized collection databases has helped this process tremendously. While card systems were arranged, at best, by three or four identifiers (e.g., accession number, artist, culture, object name), computer systems can enable searches on most words entered. If all object names, cultural affiliations, materials, artists, publishers, manufacturers and geographic origins can be easily searched, it is infinitely easier to match undocumented objects to their records than it had been before computers.

A case in point comes from the Northwest Museum of Arts and Culture (MAC), in Spokane, Washington. In 1978 the museum, then the Cheney Cowles Memorial Museum, completed its first comprehensive inventory, checking each object in the collection against a set of notebooks containing accession lists for the entire collection. At the end of the process there were more than 2000 undocumented objects and more than 2000 lost-in-inventory pieces. The reconciliation process included laying out all objects of one type (guns, Plateau material, textiles, domestic objects) and going through all lost-in-inventory descriptions to match materials with records. Perhaps a quarter of the objects were reunited with their documentation after a process that lasted more than six months.

In 1994, when the last of NAGPRA inventories was being processed, staff at the MAC came across a box of five Native American artifacts with a note from 1978 that they had not been reconciled. The database was checked for objects without location with characteristics that matched then found objects. Within an hour all were reunited with their original documentation.

Most museums assign tracking numbers to objects when they are discovered without documentation. These numbers, starting with—among many variations—N or NN (no number), X or 00 for the year, allow the museum to begin documentation without the process of accessioning approvals and decisions. Many of the state laws indicate that the process to claim ownership can be done after a museum has the object for a specific number of years. Tracking allows the museum to establish the length of time it has knowingly held the object.

If the museum uses a tracking number, however, rather than an accession number for an undocumented object, it may not be making as strong a case for ownership as it might. On the other hand, if a museum applies an accession number to an undocumented object, and thus makes a stronger ownership case, it implies that some thoughtful and careful process has been completed. The practical problems that arise from this conundrum are numerous. It is extremely difficult for museums with large, unwieldy collections to complete and reconcile inventories. It is even difficult to finish and reconcile an inventory for medium size collections, perhaps thirty to fifty thousand objects. If records are complicated and were not clearly kept, it could take years for a reconciliation process to take place.

In order to deal effectively with the problem of undocumented objects and FIC, museums should first discuss and devise policy that will provide guidance on how to proceed with undocumented versus FIC objects. If policy is not written and approved, museum staff will deal ad hoc with the problem, and the results will be uneven and confusing as changes in staff occur over the years. The policy on undocumented and FIC objects should be a subsection of the institution's acquisitions policy, approved by the institution's governing board.

The time gap between inventory and complete reconciliation must be taken into account when policy is established. It is even possible that a museum will not be able to complete an inventory, and that undocumented objects will be found from time to time during projects. Since there is so much difference of opinion on this complex and problematic subject and laws that leave little room for opinion, we present policy choices followed by a policy that we recommend be used to deal with each problem.

Museum staff should first research, with legal counsel, the laws that might deal with undocumented or FIC objects in their state. These laws may be called lost property, unclaimed property or abandoned property laws; they also may be found as sections in many of the museum-specific laws that deal primarily with old loans. If state law makes specific demands and/or denies the museum title without a claim process, the first decision is made. If it does not, the museum must devise its own procedures for assimilating FIC objects.

1. Definition

- **Undocumented objects** are those objects similar to collections and found-in-collections areas with no numbers, no information in their housing nor any characteristics that might connect them to documentation.

- **Found-in-collection** objects are undocumented objects that remain after all attempts to reconcile them to existing records of permanent collection and loan objects fail.

A list of undocumented objects should not include objects with partial documentation, objects that have numbers consistent with the museum's accession numbers (even without backup documents) or objects that have not been completely processed. A systematic process will consider how to deal with the partials, temporaries and incompletes, but documentation should exist for most of those objects. True FIC objects are those that remain after a reconciliation process without extant clues to their origin or status.

2. Different Ways that Museums Perceive Undocumented Objects

a. Museum A considers undocumented objects to be the property of the museum.

b. Museum B considers undocumented objects to be of uncertain status.

c. Museum C considers undocumented objects to be accessioned objects owned by the museum that have lost the numbers that connect them to documentation.

d. Museum D holds undocumented objects that must be processed under state museum property law in their respective state.

Unless the museum has a specific state law to follow, 2b is closest to the reality of most situations. 2a, however, is the preferred stance if the museum wishes to make the strongest claim possible on the object. Except in unusual situations, the majority of undocumented objects are owned by museums. They may be of uncertain status, but there is nothing to indicate that an undocumented object may belong to someone else; only a claim will bring that possibility forward.

There are times when a museum does know where the property came from. Consider the use of "found in collection" by the National Postal Museum: "In an attempt to fill gaps in the older issues, we have resurrected material set aside as 'duplicate' in the 1980s. We have finished the review of a selection of good mint examples from this source and have inventoried them. Their reintroduction to the collection will be complete when they are given FIC numbers and cataloged."[24] Records for the duplicate collection were obviously not as complete as those for the permanent collection, but there is reason to consider them owned by the museum.

A museum may originate from the gift of an entire estate that may include a house and its contents. Such a gift may also occur at any time; for example, the Brandywine River Museum acquired the house and studio of artist N. C. Wyeth in the 1990s. If the first sweep in the process of accessioning was not complete, and if all objects were not identified and numbered, undocumented objects and FIC objects may well be unprocessed parts of the original accession.

A second and very common scenario is a lost accession number. For example, in the 1920s some collections of Native American baskets were numbered by stapling small thick paper tags to their rims. The paper was acidic and over the years it cracked and crumbled. In some instances, the staples rusted out as well, and the baskets were left with partial tags or no tags at all. Even partial tags are a useful clue, however, since a museum worker may know the types of tags and inks used in the collection during specific time periods. The tag may even point toward a single gift. In many cases there is no way to reconcile the basket to a record, because records noting baskets in the collection may just say "coiled basket," "woven basket" or even just "basket."

The baskets without remaining identifications must be treated as undocumented objects. It is possible that they might have been loans, but a museum worker will have a sense of the proportion of loans to permanent collection objects in an individual museum, and of the type and quality of object that existed in the major collections gathered in the early days of the museum. That worker should be able to place the preponderance of the evidence with either gift/purchase or loan. In some cases, research may place the baskets as accessions or as FIC.

Museum workers are also aware of the collecting policies that were in place in the early days of their institutions. Some museums took everything that came their way, and put aside material that they felt was secondary. These secondary objects, left for future generations to deal with, are now found in collection. Sometimes they can be reconciled with some vague list; usually they can not.

Museums in small towns (perhaps from five hundred to one million or more people) have often found themselves the recipient of objects they really don't want from donors who refused to make a clear declaration of gift but wanted the museum to keep the property. Their collections may also be filled by donors who insist on giving the museum all of the bric-a-brac they own. All of the standards and policies and procedures and professional associations in the world have failed to convince directors and curators that they can risk offending the town's richest or most powerful citizen by rejecting part or parts of a gift, and as a result collections fill up with unwanted and often undocumented objects.

Almost all museums have their quirks and reasons, and almost all have undocumented and FIC objects to deal with.

3. Preliminary Actions that Museums Might Take

a. Undocumented objects will receive tracking numbers and be used in accordance with approved uses of museum collections.

b. The museum will make every attempt to reconcile undocumented objects with existing documentation, eventually considering objects that are not reconciled to be FIC.

Most museums assign tracking numbers to objects when they are discovered without documentation. This is necessary for several reasons, but primarily to avoid the process of accessioning approvals and decisions and allow immediate tracking.

Many museums, however, stop at this point. They assign tracking numbers but make no affirmative decision that the object should be in the collection; some museum policies, however, note that any object found in collection is to be considered an accessioned object.

4. Possible Decisions About FIC

a. FIC objects may be accessioned into the collection according to approved accession policy or disposed of according to approved deaccession policy.

b. Any FIC objects that might be a loan, i.e., of the object type listed in an unresolved old

loan, will be converted to museum property using applicable state law.

c. All FIC objects may be converted to museum property and then accessioned into the collection.

d. All FIC objects will be converted to museum property according to applicable state law.

During inventory reconciliation, it is common to find several objects that probably are part of an accession or an old loan, but not be able to determine for certain which of the objects were included in a given transaction. For example, after an inventory there are five dolls without numbers and documentation for four dolls that have not been found (lost in inventory). Three of those, in an accession list, are described as:

• Small cloth doll, bad condition

• Ceramic doll with blue eyes

• Doll

One doll has a loan status, and its documentation reads: "Cloth doll, 6 inches." After reviewing all the records and inspecting the dolls, it may be impossible to determine whether any of them are actually the dolls noted on the loan receipt and in the accession list. In this case, it is prudent to go through an old loan process for all the dolls, listing their source as unknown when publishing constructive notice, and accessioning (or deaccessioning) them when that process is complete. The documentation remains, the objects listed as lost-in-inventory unless and until more information is found.

FIC objects are often inferior to already accessioned objects. Constraints on staff time generally translate into taking more care to document and track objects that are considered very valuable. Lesser objects receive less time and less documentation. While some FIC material may be considered relevant to the mission of the museum, not affirming it by accessioning when it originally arrived is a major indicator that it never fit, and should be processed out of the museum. The process of dealing with FIC objects presents the ideal time to review each object, affirm or reject it and, if affirmed, to process it into the collection.

Accessioning the object implies that it may be used in the same way other museum objects are used: that it may be exhibited, loaned, photographed, published, conserved or deaccessioned. If FIC objects receive tracking numbers rather than accession numbers, the museum's policy should state that tracked FIC objects may also be used in accordance with policies and procedures covering accessioned objects.

5. Ways to Accession FIC Material

a. The process of accessioning FIC objects will begin with:
  • A decision of the director and curator
  • A decision of the curator and/or
  • Review by the acquisitions committee of the museum.

b. FIC objects will be accessioned into the permanent collection following all steps in the museum's acquisitions (or accessions) policy.

c. The assignment of a number to the object when it is found will indicate that it is accessioned.

d. FIC acquisitions will (or will not) be reported in the annual report.

If a museum takes the approach that FIC objects are already theirs and that there is institutional evidence to believe that most FIC objects were simply missed or have lost their documents, the process of accessioning may be the more internal affirmation (curator or curator/director) in options a. Reporting accessions with an FIC source, however, is important so that collection size and sources are updated and transparent. It may be, as well, another source of notice that would make the museum's case stronger. The museum might also require that an affidavit be signed and dated by either the person assigning the original tracking number or by a curator or other staff member with knowledge of possible owner-

ship, e.g., recollection of a group of objects coming in together or knowledge of the type of material that appeared in an early collection.

6. Options for Deaccession

Whether or not an accessioning process is completed, deaccessioning should follow the approved policy so that all parties are aware of the object's legal status and the potential risk of disposing of it.

a. FIC objects slated for disposition will follow the deaccession process as if they are owned, permanent collection objects.

b. FIC objects slated for deaccession will be claimed under applicable state law before deaccessioning takes place.

c. FIC objects will be claimed under applicable state law before they are either accessioned or deaccessioned.

There is no evidence, with FIC objects, that the museum does not own the object. Ildiko DeAngelis, former Smithsonian counsel and currently director of the George Washington University museum studies program, has stated:

Legally, actually, you're in a much better position with FICs than you are with old loans, because the undisturbed possession by the museum of this object, often for decades, is in itself evidence that supports a presumption that the title is owned by the museum. In other words, because you own it and you possess it, and you lack evidence that it's not yours, the law gives you a break. It actually is on your side.

The burden of proof would be on anyone who wants to claim that object as theirs. In other words, the museum can sit there on its laurels and say, this is ours, prove to us otherwise. So the claimant has the burden of proof, and honestly, that burden is often heavy.[25]

DeAngelis holds that the accession number is far better than a tracking number in the event that a claim for title is made. She notes that getting rid of FIC complies with the responsibilities of a museum that holds objects in the public trust.

If a museum adds an FIC object to its permanent collection, the worst that can happen is a future claim, the potential success of which will diminish as time passes. If a successful claim is made, the worst that can happen is the return of an object to its rightful owner. The museum might even negotiate a gift, if the situation warrants it.

If a museum disposes of an object by sale, it does open itself up to penalty should a successful claim ever be made. Each state's version of the Uniform Commercial Code applies, and if a successful claim is made, the museum may have to pay the current value of the object, rather than the value for which the object was sold. If instead the museum donates the object, or sells it with notice of flawed title (in all likelihood reducing the price), there is less recourse for the owner whose claim has succeeded. Review Malaro's text on claims,[26] applicable state law and the risk chart on page 48.

7. Possible Actions if Original Documentation is Found or a Claim is Made

a. If original documentation is found for an object that has been tracked or accessioned into the collection using an FIC number, it will be returned to its original number and the FIC number will be retired.

b. If a claim is made on an FIC object, either accessioned into the collection or disposed of, the museum will make ad hoc decisions on accepting or fighting the claim.

If a claim is made, the museum must request proof that the object claimed from the collection is the object described in the claimant's documents, and that the claimant is either the sole owner or that he or she has complete authority from all of the owners to make the claim. The first part may require very precise documentation, e.g., a "flowered vase" will hardly describe one of five vases of different periods made of different materials that exist in the collection with FIC documentation only. It may also be difficult for a person to claim that he or she is the only heir. It is common for more than one person to inherit from an estate. If this is compounded, the longer a museum has held an object, the less the chance of a successful claim.

The museum must respond to a claim as soon as is feasible. If the proof is strong, the museum should return the object quickly. If the proof is weak, the museum should reject the claim in writing. This starts a statute of limitations (usually three to six years) to bring a suit against the museum. If a suit is filed, the museum may decide whether to fight the claim or return the object—this, too, is often dependent on the value and uniqueness of the object.

Putting the preferred policy parts together, we offer the following models for policy and procedures:

Policy on Undocumented and Found-in-Collection Objects

Undocumented objects are those objects similar to collections and found-in-collections areas with no numbers, no information in their housing nor any characteristics that might connect them to documentation. Found-in-collection (FIC) objects are undocumented objects that remain without status after all attempts to reconcile them to existing records of permanent collection and loan objects fail.

The museum will make every attempt to reconcile undocumented objects to existing documentation. Objects that are not reconciled will be considered FIC.

The museum considers undocumented and FIC objects to be the property of the museum. Undocumented objects will be tracked and documented from the time they are found, and may be used as any permanent collection object is used. FIC objects may be accessioned into the collection or disposed of according to approved deaccession policy. The registrar is responsible for tracking numbers, and for bringing FIC objects to the attention of the curator. The decision to accession may be made by the curator with the approval of the director, as documented on an acquisition proposal form. FIC objects accessioned into the permanent collection will be given numbers in the year of accession and included in the annual report of objects.

If original documentation is found for an object that has been tracked or accessioned into the collection using an FIC number, the object will be returned to its original status and number and the FIC number will be retired.

If a claim is made on an undocumented or FIC object, either accessioned into the collection or disposed of, the museum will make ad hoc decisions on accepting or fighting the claim.

Unclaimed objects and FIC objects slated for disposition will follow the approved deaccession process as if they are permanent collection objects.

Procedures

1. Assign and apply a tracking number.

Objects without documentation should be assigned a number immediately.

If the number is to serve as both a tracking number and an accession number (that is, museum policy considers all undocumented objects to be FIC property of the museum from the time they are found), it is preferable to put it at the beginning of the year's accessions. If an accession number, it should follow the same pattern used for all of the museum's accessions. Example:

2007.00.1

An accession group with the source "Unknown" is given 00. It could as easily be 0 or 000, depending on the numbering system used by the museum. It may be stronger to dispense with the 00 entirely, and give the FIC the next number in line, i.e., 2007.1.1. Again, one number can be used for all of the FIC objects accessioned in the calendar year.

If the number is simply for tracking, and decisions about accessioning are to be made after some review, the number might be a reverse of the usual accession number. With a standard tripartite system, for example, the first undocumented object of the year might be:

00.2007.1

The sequence can continue throughout the year, with museum staff adding as many objects as found, i.e., 00.2007.2, 00.2007.3, etc. In 2008, 00.2008 is reserved for FIC accessions.

Museums have used a variety of tracking systems to indicate undocumented objects: numbers prefixed by X or N, 00 numbers followed only by sequential numbers and prefixes used on a yearly basis, for example.

It is not advisable, especially with a numbering system that will probably see many retired numbers, to change what exists in records already created. It is advisable, however, to alter the system slightly for the present and future if a year is not indicated in the existing number system. Various state laws make it important to be able to prove how long an object has been in the museum if a claim is made. The number can serve as part of that proof. It is also important because of the constraints on staff time in most museums; the process may not get past the numbering stage for years or even decades.

Current system: 00.1, 00.2, 00.3, etc.
Change to: 00.2007.1, 00.2007.2, etc., then 00.2008.1, etc., for the next year.

Current system: N1, N2, N3, etc.
Change to: N2007.1, N2007.2, etc., then N2008.1, etc., for the next year.

The number assigned may be applied immediately, using the same methods used to number a permanent collection object. Whereas loans are not usually permanently marked, both undocumented and FIC objects may be. Or the object may be tagged during inventory reconciliation and a permanent physical number applied only after it is reconciled and accessioned as an FIC object.

2. Gather basic registration information.

- Description
- Measurement
- Condition report
- Photograph

Describe all undocumented objects in the system used for recording permanent collections. For most museums, this has become a computerized collections database from which a catalogue card can be printed. Using the database or a regular worksheet, measure the object. Complete a condition report. Collect and record as much information as can be taken from the object itself, particularly information about any marks, collector's numbers or other characteristics that can differentiate it from other objects. Photograph the object, and if possible, put a photo in the computer, on the printout of the catalogue card or on the manually produced catalogue card, and/or in the object folder.

3. Complete an institutional search for information.

Record comments from staff members who might remember details about the object for the FIC object file. For example, the director might have seen the object at a particular time or remembers using it in an exhibition a decade before it is "found." Perhaps a curator or a registrar remembers bringing in a group of similar materials and believes that the object in question is a part of that group. A nondescript mark or number on the object may ring a bell with someone aware of the habits of a certain collector who marked his or her

objects in a particular way.

Write down any information that is found, and sign and date the document. Melinda Simms, as part of her master's thesis "Found in Collections: Reconciling Undocumented Objects in Historical Museums," devised an affidavit form to use for formalizing the information gathered. Such a document adds to the strength of the museum's claim of ownership (see appendix B).

4. Reconcile undocumented objects with lost-in-inventory objects.

Inventory reconciliation is the process of matching objects to documentation; for undocumented objects, it is the more complicated process of trying to match objects without numbers to documentation without objects. It is generally and most easily accomplished with the aid of a complete inventory. Trying to find a single object without a good catalogue, preferably entered into a computerized database, can be one of the most frustrating collection tasks possible. The process of reconciling FIC objects is best done as the final part of a reconciled inventory. Records of objects that have not been found in that inventory are prime candidates for matches with un-numbered objects.

Chapter 4 on the Northwest Museum of Art and History gives an example of how manual records were used for the process. If a collections database is available, first make certain that there is at least a "place-holder" file for each object noted in either catalogue cards or accession ledger, and keep track of all moves in the database. Over time, even without a complete inventory, locations are noted and a history of where objects have been and are currently located emerges. Databases allow easy searches for objects named but with no location. For example, a rifle is found in the collection and a computerized search for rifles that have no known locations yields a list of perhaps five examples with which to begin comparisons.

This process is long and arduous. It can sometimes be done in pieces, i.e., locate and inventory every doll in the collection. Find all of the doll records. Compare them all. It is even better if this step can be done before any numbers are assigned, in order to avoid the necessity of retiring tracking or mistaken accession numbers. Such an ideal sequence, however, generally cannot and does not happen unless there is ample and dedicated staff to work on the specific project.

Lost in Inventory

Conundrum!

When is a "lost-in-inventory" object truly lost in inventory?

Never. Although one can never be certain an object is truly lost, a museum may decide to claim the loss on their insurance policy after a careful check of all areas where the object might reasonably be (storage, conservation, exhibition, loan) and after checking with all staff who might have had reason to interact with the object. A new inventory of suspect areas and records should find the object or leave staff relatively certain that it has been inadvertently disposed of or stolen. Records for lost property should never be removed from files or databases.

5. For reconciled objects, affirm and apply original number. Retire tracking number.

Keep a record on the object's card, in its file and/or in its computer record, of the tracking number that was assigned to it. It is not always possible to eliminate or change all of the records where a number was used. That tracking number will pop up somewhere and will need to be linked to the current object number.

6. For remaining objects, decide whether to accession or dispose.

The museum's policy will outline the process for making this decision. The registrar or collections manager who is working on the FIC objects should alert the curator responsible for a particular collection when it is determined that an object is truly without documentation. Decision to accession or dispose can be made in accordance

with the guidelines for accession or deaccession outlined in the museum's collection management policy and in accordance with the process outlined in the policy for FIC objects.

Review the FIC object to determine if any federal or state laws regarding materials or origin affect the status of the object. If this has not already been done when the FIC object was found, check whether the object is covered under the Native American Graves Protection and Repatriation Act, the Endangered Species Act or other laws that control the use and movement of species or specific types of material taken from them. If a curator knows of possible stolen or looted objects, or objects removed from their countries in violation of laws in place, the museum may move to restore or repatriate as well.

7. Accession the FIC object.

Add the object to the permanent system as if it were an object on approval from any other source. Change the number (see 1 above) and record the object in the current year. Should this object be deaccessioned in the future, it should be deaccessioned in accordance with the deaccession policy in place, and its former FIC status should be noted and used to make decisions regarding the risk the museum is taking. If the museum pursues title to FIC objects before deaccessioning, that policy would apply.

8. Dispose of an undocumented or FIC object.

Undocumented and FIC objects are in their most sensitive moment when they are deaccessioned. Regardless of whether the object was accessioned or just tracked, it is imperative that the complete deaccessioning process in accordance with the museum's policy be used to dispose of it. Trustees must know if there is a risk of future claims against the museum. As noted on the risk chart below, it is likely that objects that are multiples, of small or no monetary value or given to other not-for-profit institutions pose little or no risk. The museum may not have the time, staff or resources to use legal processes to convert small or minor objects. Consider, for example, how many Sears and Roebuck cast-iron irons will be claimed and whether they are worth a lawsuit. Even differentiating among five irons catalogued briefly as "clothes irons" may not be possible. Use common sense, and document everything very carefully.

The risk for unique objects, especially those of high value, is a different matter. Legal counsel should be sought, and using available laws to take title to the property may prove a positive factor in fighting future claims.

UNSOLICITED DEPOSITS

Unsolicited deposits may come to the museum with or without a known or identifiable owner. A short statement on dealing with unsolicited deposits should be placed in the acquisition policy. When the owner is known, it is sometimes possible to return unwanted property. When that information is incomplete, or the owner is not known, decisions are more complex.

Museums may receive property through the mail; handed to a security guard, shop clerk or volunteer; or literally left on the doorstep without ownership identity or documented intention for disposition. This type of property has been referred to as a "doorstep donation."[27] Some examples of the types of "abandoned property" many museums encounter are:

a. A man appears at the loading dock of a museum with an antique fire extinguisher and tells the security guard that he is leaving it for the fire museum collection. The security guard, ignoring or ignorant of policy, takes the fire extinguisher, asks for no information and puts it aside. Eventually it finds its way to the collections division of the museum.

b. A woman approaches the information desk at a museum and pushes a bag toward the attendant. She says nothing and hurries away. The attendant looks in the bag, finds two necklaces of African origin and, knowing that the museum does not accept objects casually and at minimum needs information, goes after the owner. That person has disappeared. A curator later decides that the necklaces, which are of good quality, were probably part of a spiritual dilemma and that the person felt it was detrimental to continue to own them. The curator proceeds to accession them.

Deaccession Risk Chart

MOST RISK	Value	Disposition Method	Clarity of title	Object Type
	$1 million +		clouded title	unique
		destroy	undocumented/FIC	
		return to source	accession number only	small series
		sell privately	unsigned deed of gift (no value)	
		sell at auction	unclear documentation	limited edition, artist
		exchange	object and/or source card file	
		repatriate	annual reports	limited edition, manufactured
		give to nonprofit	report to trustees	
LEAST RISK	$0	internal transfer	countersigned deed of gift/intent	mass-produced (man-made)
			acknowledgment/clear bill of sale	abundant (natural)

Doorstep Donations
Ildiko DeAngelis

To complete a gift and thereby receive good title, you need:

a. An offer from the donor

b. Acceptance from the donee

c. Transfer of control (delivery)

With doorstep donations, the circumstances involved with dropping something off at the doorstep of the museum can reasonably be interpreted as an offer and delivery. If the museum decides to accept the object, transfer of title is complete and the museum's title should be clear.

While it is true the museum does not know who the donor might have been, that should not affect the quality of the title, only the quality of the museum's documentation of its title. I can understand that good documentation is so embedded into collections managers that the lack of clear documentation makes everyone nervous. However, recommending the step of going through a title clearance procedure offered by state old loan laws for doorstep donation is, in my opinion, overkill.

Instead, I would recommend that the museum create detailed internal records of how the object was received (listing all the details of the "offer" and "deliver") and documentation of the "acceptance" and then proceed to accession or process the artifact as with any other gift.

If in the highly unlikely chance that a person comes by sometime in the future and says "I lost my grandmother's rocking chair on your sidewalk," then the museum can deal with that on a case by case basis. The burden of proof would be on the claimant. I think it would be better to deal with a problem like that as it comes up, rather than going through a time-consuming process for objects to which the museum, under basic law of gifts, should have legal title.

For doorstep donations, more so than for most FICs, we will know when and the circumstances of how it came to the museum. We can and should use those facts to the museum's advantage.

It is not necessary to accept such donations, of course, and the disposition of them will depend on value, condition and usefulness to the museum. Live animals must be tended to immediately and if the museum is not equipped to care for them turned over to the SPCA or county animal welfare agency. Items which will spoil or rot, such as food or live flowers, should be thrown away at once.

Materials in which the museum has no interest should be discarded in the manner best suited to the object in question. An item of aesthetic or historic interest outside the collecting parameters of the museum might be given to another not-for-profit institution or sold at auction for the benefit of the museum's collection. Items of lesser value might be sold at a museum benefit tag sale or simply thrown away.

Doorstep donations that would enhance the museum's collection should be handled as found-in-collection objects: numbered, accessioned and treated as permanent collection. Prudence dictates waiting an established period of time, such as 90 days or 6 months, to be sure the owner does not reappear to claim the property. Due diligence might entail a more concerted effort to identify and contact the donor; publication for two or three weeks of the museum's intention to claim ownership of the described property in a newspaper of general circulation in the county where the museum is located is a wise step if budget permits. Such action would strengthen the museum's ownership position in the event of a future claim from the previous owner.

Whatever action the museum takes should be fully documented and a record including description and photograph of the object, the circumstances of its acquisition and the manner of its disposition kept for future reference.

Memorial collections are frequently made from objects left in remembrance. Such collections are left at sites of intense emotional concentration: war memorials and places where tragedies occurred are examples. The National Park Service oversees collections from the Vietnam Veterans

Memorial, Oklahoma City's Alfred P. Murrah Federal Building, the Columbine shooting site and the Flight 93 Memorial in Shanksville, Pennsylvania. The New York Historical Society cares for material from the 9-11 World Trade Center site, and the Center for Military History manages objects left at the site of the 9-11 Pentagon explosions.

The United States Holocaust Memorial Museum received large numbers of objects after its opening in 1993, but that number has dropped as years have gone by. The material they kept was accessioned as permanent collection material. If something is left at the New Jersey Vietnam Veteran's Memorial, however, it becomes part of the Memorial Collection, which is tracked separately from the permanent collection. The New Jersey Vietnam Veterans Memorial does not accept material casually dropped off at the museum and makes attempts to return it to the depositor, if known. In order to be part of the Memorial Collection, an object must be left at the memorial.

Objects of remembrance must be reviewed and problems culled. Live flowers have to be disposed of and the contents of cans discarded. The beer can without the beer becomes a memorial object.[28] The national Vietnam Veterans Memorial has more than 100,000 objects that were collected at the Wall (and not from the traveling memorials), which are numbered and tracked separately from all other objects in the National Park Service collection. Mailed material is not accepted, nor is material that is carried to the offices. The Vietnam Veterans Memorial collection is exhibited all over the world, but the vast majority of the objects are in storage. All are cared for according to museum standards, documented and stored in a climate-controlled environment.

The composition of the material presents many conservation problems. The collection of the Vietnam Veterans Memorial includes everything from wreaths, flags, uniforms and teddy bears to a six-foot stained-glass soldier and a unique, hand-built Harley Davidson. The motorcycle

was made by the Wisconsin Vietnam Veterans to commemorate POW-MIA. Families and friends leave arts and craft pieces, photographs, poker chips and crosses. Pam West, regional curator, who advocated for the collection's care and is in charge of it, says that a second type of object is now being left at the site: objects related to free speech, protest and advocacy.

For institutions dealing with this type of collection, unsolicited deposits are no small problem but reflect the core of the mission. Most of the procedures they use are uniform. They receive objects either as mail-in/walk-in donations or as left at memorials. They refuse the former and accept the latter, which are more often direct responses to individuals memorialized than to the event the memorial represents. The memorials are considered property of the institution and are documented, cared for and used in accordance with the mission.

Eventually it is likely that fewer objects will be left at the current sites, as at the Holocaust Museum. If the leaving of objects continues to be strong, it is likely that policies will be established to discontinue collecting all of the memorials. The potential for growth of these collections and the cost of their care are overwhelming.

FINDING LENDERS, DONORS AND ARTISTS

People get lost in the veil of time.[29] Lenders disappear without forwarding addresses; donors move away; artists go from place to place. In death, the legal obligations and rights held by all pass through their estates to others who are often unaware of specific contracts and obligations that exist. Museums must find lenders when the time comes to return loaned materials. They must find donors when a deed of gift is discovered to be incomplete or unsigned. They must find artists when the need to obtain copyright license arises.

Marie Malaro, author of *A Legal Primer on Managing Museum Collections* and a leading museum ethicist, discusses pursuing a "good faith and reasonable search," a phrase that is open to interpretation. Kathryn Speckart, collections manager, US Diplomacy Center, United States Department of State, in a lecture on old loans, explains that "a 'good faith' search means the researcher was honest, fair, and lawful in their attempt to locate the lender or heirs." The depth and intensity of a search depends, in part, on the importance placed on the object. If an object is a very important, high value old loan and the museum wishes very strongly to convert it to gift, the whole gamut of searches can be run. If a low value duplicate object is to be disposed of, actual and constructive notices, as required by state law, may be enough to satisfy the museum's needs and protect its interests.

The traditional method of locating a person involves searching diligently through museum files for any indications of the person, clues about times and places and leads to close personal ties. Once an address is found, then actual notice—a certified letter with delivery notification—can be sent to determine whether a person is known at a specific address. Even if the donor must logically be deceased because of the date of the transaction, it is possible that a relative still resides at the address. If the person is known, the problem can usually be resolved. If the person is not known, or if the address has disappeared, further research is necessary.

Those next steps involve finding other persons or institutions that might have information about the sought-after person. Traditional sources of information include telephone directories, city directories and, of course, the archives of local newspapers. These sources may lead to court records—vital records, wills and land transactions—and then to clubs and businesses. If the person is not found, an heir might be located.

All of the people in the general area with the same last name can be contacted. It is sometimes possible to track moves from one part of town to another through city directories, phone books and land records. For artists, a *Who's Who* volume might hold further information.

The better known the person, the easier he or she is to find. Most donors and lenders, and many artists, are not well known. If there is an article in a local paper, it is likely to be an obituary, and obituaries hold good clues. For instance, if a man was an Elks Club member, then the Elks can be contacted, or perhaps he worked at the local university where records probably exist. A spouse or other survivors can be traced in the same manner as the deceased.

An obituary also provides time and place of death, which leads to a county courthouse with probate records. The records of the court are public, and wills can be found and read once the proper location is found. It is also possible to obtain, as all genealogists know, death certificates, which list addresses, spouses and parents. In fact, one of the best tools in researching lost people is a genealogical primer. The methods are the same, though the motives are not. The joy of the twenty-first century is that much of this searching can be done through readily available Internet resources.

The advent of the Internet has provided a new arena in which to search for individuals. Start with the person's name. Typing it into a good search engine such as Google might yield a dozen leads. The Registrars Committee of the American Association of Museums lists reference material with updates of laws, websites and recommended methods of searching (www.rcaam.org).[30]

It is also possible to find business listings under the Secretary of State's website, with a contact for extant businesses. There are, as well, sites that offer paid searches for missing people.

If following all the search suggestions above does not yield evidence of the original person or their heirs, the museum can resolve old loans and problematic donations by publishing constructive notice. Whether it does this, and the way it is done, will depend upon state law; it is best to consult legal counsel about state requirements prior to starting such processes.

Situation	Website type
1. To confirm that the lender has actually died	Genealogy; vital records; obituaries
2. To find possible heirs to the lender	Public records (probate); obituaries
3. To confirm lender lives at an address	Telephone directories; public records
4. To find or confirm any information on lender	Search engines

Finding an Artist

Virginia O'Hara

A large group of drawings was found under floorboards of a studio formerly owned by the artists Earle and Henrietta ("Pete") Miller. The studio was part of an estate donated to the Brandywine Conservancy, Brandywine River Museum's parent organization, so the drawings were brought to the curatorial department for examination and possible accession into the collection. A majority of the drawings, prints and paintings were created by the former owners, but some were by other artists. Among these was a portfolio of lithographs entitled *Thirteen Ways of Looking at a Blackbird,* signed by the artist, David Umholtz, and dated 1967. As the museum focuses on 19th- and early 20th-century American art, the staff was unfamiliar with Umholtz and his work. Research was needed before deciding whether to retain the portfolio and to determine its value for insurance purposes.

While the museum library provides strong support for study related to the museum's collection it was unlikely to contain resources for contemporary printmakers. Instead, the staff used the Internet and specifically Google's search engine to look for the artist's name and quickly found Umholtz connected to exhibitions at numerous galleries and printmaking organizations. When selected, the website of the Society of American Graphic Artists displayed an article written in 2004 about a new print studio on Staten Island that invited fourteen printmakers to test new Bavarian limestones for use in lithography. Among the fourteen, Umholtz, noted as being from Deer Island, Nova Scotia, was one of two non-New York artists who participated. Given this new information, focus shifted to Canadian websites. A website for a college in Newfoundland displayed a print by the artist and provided the artist's place and date of birth in Pennsylvania, his education

and place of residence in New Brunswick, Canada. Google listed a website for the Open Studio in Toronto that showed examples of Umholtz's current work. Unfortunately, the gallery was closed for the month of August so further inquiries there had to wait.

A simple search using online white pages provided contact information for the artist, and a voicemail message to him identified the museum's purpose. A few days later, the artist telephoned to confirm his creation of the portfolio while an intern at the former Print Club, now the Print Center, in Philadelphia, during his student days at the University of Pennsylvania. He had made the prints in an edition of ten but had no recollection that they had ever been distributed or knowledge of how they came into the Millers' hands. The artist generously mailed the museum an outline of his career and suggested that the Canadian Gallery, Open Studio, might be able to assist in determining the portfolio's value. The museum also contacted the Print Center but found their archives to be uncatalogued and in offsite storage, not easily retrieved. Thus, we could not pursue further information about Umholtz's work as a student, nor ascertain the Millers' possible connection with the Print Club that may have led to their acquisition of the portfolio. The Print Center was helpful in providing local contacts for print appraisals.

The Internet, in this case, was convenient and helpful in quickly providing information about the artist and his work. While using the Internet for research can at times result in information that is too basic or unreliable, it just as often offers researchers additional clues and surprisingly accessible resources. While it is not a substitute for consulting library and archival materials, it is a tool that, for some subjects, can be used productively in tandem with more traditional research methods.

MINOR CONUNDRUMS

1. Clear Title for Gifts

The question of what constitutes a clear title for a gift comes up often when museum workers are discussing collection problems. There are three conditions that must be met to make the transfer of title final:

- Donor intent
- Museum acceptance
- Physical receipt of object(s) by museum

Donor intent and museum acceptance are most easily executed by having both parties sign and date a deed of gift. If a deed of gift is not executed, a letter of intent and a letter of acknowledgment serve the same purpose. A receipt for the object should indicate the date the object arrived at the museum. That date may be important for IRS purposes as well as for museum reports.

2. Title for Objects of Various Use

It is usual for gifts, bequests and purchases on approval to come to the museum and be issued a temporary receipt (incoming receipt) indicating their status. Decisions about the disposition of objects on approval should be made in a timely fashion after they have arrived at a museum; the decision should be at least within the calendar year so that possible tax issues may be addressed.

Objects that have come in as bequests or gifts on approval may be accepted for the permanent collection. They may also be accepted and designated for use outside the permanent collection. Objects may be destined for a loan collection, sale, an educational, hands-on collection or use by the museum. That decision should be made and indicated on the title transfer paperwork.

It is prudent to include on a deed of gift only those objects intended for permanent collections. If objects not for the permanent collection are accepted, it is absolutely necessary to flag them and state clearly on the deed of gift that they are meant

for the loan collection, or study and student use in a secondary collection, etc. Curators must make decisions about the destination of objects before the transfer of title is complete so that the donors are aware of the destinations as well and know how their donations will serve the institution.

If an object is acquired for sale or use, the transaction is best handled by a department other than a collections department. They might use a letter and an acknowledgment. At times, because of value and handling knowledge, collections staff are asked to hold objects not intended for the permanent collections. Objects with this status should be clearly marked and the practice kept to a minimum.

3. Unsigned Gift Agreements

Coming across an unsigned gift agreement in the files, a museum worker should note first whether it was intended to be left unsigned or whether the donor never returned the signed deed of gift.

If the lack of signature was intentional, the museum might defend its ownership through general business records that indicate that the gift was intended on the basis of an oral contract. Perhaps this "no signature needed" gift is similar to a no signature loan, in which either the borrower, the amount or both pose a low risk and allow less red tape. Waiver of signature was probably intended to make gifts of small value easier to complete. Although there are values below which federal courts will not hear cases, state courts recognize no such limits, and the museum must determine its best course of action if challenged on a small-value gift. Most likely, return of the low value gift will not make a major impact on the collection.

If the donor never returned the signed deed of gift, look for letters of intent and acceptance. Museums often have problematic transactions, and donors sometimes refuse to sign a deed of gift even after everything seems to be settled. If the problem is current, work with the donor to soothe the problems and if nothing can be done, return the property. The person who will not give the property completely is the person who will ask for it back long after it has been left with the museum, and the problems at that time will probably have increased.

If the problem is old, send a new deed of gift to the current address and reopen the transaction. If the donor is no longer at that address, assess the risk to the museum and if the risk is high, search out the donor as you would for an old loan or, if the risk is minimal, let the gift lie.

4. Incomplete Deeds of Gift

For both unsigned and incomplete gift agreements, look carefully for letters of intent and letters of acknowledgment. Registrars can become focused on deeds of gift and overlook the correspondence that also proves ownership. If a deed of gift lacks a signature or omits an object or objects, proceed by sending a new deed of gift or by sending a letter itemizing the objects that were included and asking the donor to affirm his of her gift. They might countersign the letter or write their own letter affirming intent.

If the donor has moved, initiate a search after assessing risk, as above, to determine whether there is adequate probability of claim to justify staff time.

5. No Written Records for Early Gifts

Museums that reach back into the 1800s or even early 1900s may have few records for early collections. Even when records exist, there are few written indications that a gift was made. If the museum worker is lucky, a bound ledger may show date of receipt, intent, name of depositor, address and a brief description of the objects involved. Many early transactions undertaken by museums were oral, and the visible evidence that remains is a group of objects that have accession numbers, have been treated as gifts and may have at least an initial ledgerbook entry.

As intent does not always take written form, neither does acceptance. Looking for proof of title for old collections can become an exercise in historical detective work. It is a good exercise to chart the museum's documentation history to help determine status. A combination of ledgers, letters, receipts,

even strange notations on cards, can help disclose the true status of an object and the value it was perceived to have when it arrived.

For example, if a museum object has been in the collection for forty years, was assigned an accession number those long years ago and was noted in a ledger or in an object file as a gift, there is good cause to believe it is the property of the museum even though neither letters nor deed of gift exists. Acceptance is implied by the assignment of the accession number and by the physical presence of the object in the museum. Intent is not as clear, but the museum worker of the time wrote "gift" and obviously believed that to be the status. If all gifts were processed in a similar manner, there is good evidence that the object is a gift. A claim against that status would have to be very strong and very concrete.

A Missouri lawyer explains how an oral contract might be proven if a challenge to ownership in that state is made:

> *The question may be, "Is evidence of a parol gift admissible?" and if so, "What evidence exists?" In Missouri, and I think all states, certain evidence may be admissible even without a written agreement. For example, in Missouri, there is (among other tools a recipient may use) a Business Records Act. Briefly, a record of an act, condition, or event shall, insofar as relevant, be competent evidence if the custodian or other qualified witness testifies to its identity and the mode of its preparation, if it was made in the regular course of business, at or near the time of the act, condition, or event, and if, in the opinion of the court, the sources of information, method, and time of preparation were such as to justify its admission.*[31]

Most museum workers could testify to the types of numbering systems, the ink and even the handwriting that appears in early records and on objects. They could further testify that these methods were common for museum business at the time. In many cases, even the person who made the records could be named. So in addition to all of the other things that museums workers must know, a sound knowledge of the institution's historical documentation may prove most valuable.

6. Shared Ownership

Occasionally, and usually only under exceptional circumstances, museums share ownership of an object or a work of art. There are many reasons for such an arrangement: a donor may have close bonds with both institutions; the cost may be so high that sharing is the only way to purchase the object; it may be a solution to a title dispute; or, it may be a negotiated settlement when the object is vital to the missions of two institutions. It may, of course, be whimsy as well.

Fractional gifts are those which are given over a period of time; the museum and the donor usually intend that the museum will eventually have complete ownership of the property. Similar in terms of contract, but different in outcome, are the shared ownership situations where the museum enters into an ownership agreement that will always be partial.

When an offer for partial ownership is made, and the museum decides to accept a percentage of the object, two contracts must be drawn. The first is the transfer of title from the vendor or donor; the second is a contract of understanding outlining use and responsibilities of the two owners. The second contract must outline responsibilities for storage, shipping, lending, rights and reproduction, conservation, insurance and exhibition. It usually guides the amount of time each institution will hold the object, and the permissions that are necessary when the object is loaned, conserved or published.

Objects of shared ownership pose the same tracking problems that plague both partial gifts and restricted gifts. The museum must be aware of its responsibilities and must follow through on the promises that have been made. Charting all objects with complex use restrictions, as well as flagging them on a computer database and checking files whenever objects are considered for exhibition, loan, conservation or publication, allows the museum worker to fulfill the museum's legal obligations.

The Bradford Cup
Jeanne M. Benas

A silver drinking cup made in London in 1634 and once belonging to William Bradford, the second governor of Plymouth Colony, was jointly purchased by the Smithsonian Institution and the Pilgrim Society in 1985. The Bradford cup is exhibited at either the Smithsonian's National Museum of American History or the Pilgrim Hall Museum every three years.

The joint "Agreement for Purchase and Sale of the William Bradford Cup and For Its Subsequent Disposition and Display" was drafted by a Smithsonian attorney and approved by both museums. The agreement outlines conditions of the sale, the amount paid by each museum, the terms of ownership including shipping and insurance and other general terms. Each museum insures the cup "during the time it is in their care, custody, and control, including transit."[32] The museum shipping the cup pays packing and shipping expenses. General terms such as the responsibility for paying indirect expenses by the museum incurring them (e.g., curatorial salaries, utilities, security and general overhead), the responsibility for direct expenses to be paid by both museums jointly (e.g., cost of insurance, permissible repairs or restorations), and required permissions for the conservation, preservation or cleaning by both museums are standard conditions of a loan. "Neither [museum] may unilaterally deaccession, sell, donate, encumber or otherwise affect its ownership interest, nor take any steps which purport to so affect the ownership interest of the other [museum]."[33] The reproduction of the cup for commercial purposes and the loan of the cup to a third party museum can occur as long as the decision is mutually agreed upon by both museums.

The logic of the agreement follows the logic of an outgoing loan, except this outgoing loan will continue in perpetuity. As a result, we gain ongoing visibility for one of the treasures of the National Museum of American History.

7. Gifts of Fractional Interest

Donors often want to give the museum only a fractional interest in a work of art or artifact; this gift of fractional interest has been a time-honored way of spreading tax deductibility over several years. It has also allowed a donor to give an asset to the museum while retaining ownership and possession of it for a portion of the year. The Pension Protection Act of 2006, signed into law on August 17, 2006, changed fractional gifts dramatically.

Deeds of fractional gift have traditionally been developed on an ad hoc basis between museum and donor. A 10 percent portion might be given, for instance, with another 10 percent to come every year or every other year. It has always been in the interest of the museum to press a donor to give all of the remaining interest at a specific rate, at a definite time or upon the donor's death. The Pension Protection Act, however, spells out specific time limits—ten years for full donation—and it also regulates appraisals and sets specific allowable deductions.

The museum community lobbied against many of the charitable gift provisions of the Pension Protection Act, and were unsuccessful in some areas. AAM and the Association of Art Museum Directors (AAMD) continue to lobby; the regulations have not been developed as of April 2007 and there are many questions remaining about implementation. It is imperative that museums do not enter into fractional gifts without a full reading of the new laws, and that they become aware of the effect of the current law (and future changes) on deeds of fractional interest that are already in process.

Fractional gifts should be accessioned and assigned a number in the year in which the first fractional interest is given. The registrar must monitor such gifts carefully. A flag on the computer record, a note on the calendar or another reliable "tickler" mechanism will serve as a reminder to modify records to reflect additional percentage ownership as appropriate, and to make transfer arrangements for the annual term of physical possession.

8. Gifts in Community Property States

The Washington State Bar Association discusses the community property laws of the state of Washington as follows:

> In Washington, husband and wife are a "marital community" and, once married, the earnings of each are "community property." Under this system, all property acquired from earnings during marriage (such as real estate, automobiles or household goods) belongs equally to husband and wife, even when only one is employed.[34] Debts as well as assets are equally divided.

In addition to Washington, community property laws exist in Arizona, California, Idaho, Louisiana, Nevada, New Mexico, Texas and Wisconsin. A museum sitting in one of these nine states should require that all deeds of gift from married couples be signed by both spouses. If the museum accepts the property from only one spouse, it may be open to litigation from the nonsigning spouse who claims the material as community property in the marriage.

Although laws differ from state to state, and may not cover property inherited or held by an individual before marriage, it is better not to guess about ownership. The alternative to both signatures is to investigate the particular property involved and to consult attorneys, a complicated and expensive route. The Los Angeles County Museum of Art, located in a community property state, simply requires signatures from both spouses. The risk for a museum is lowered in all cases of donation by a married person, regardless of the state, if both spouses sign transfers for the property.

Community Property States
(as of 2005)

Arizona

California

Idaho

Louisiana

Nevada

New Mexico

Texas

Wisconsin

Washington

9. Promised Gifts

Potential donors often promise gifts to museums. The promise may come as a future bequest, as a promise to give the remainder of a fractional gift or as a vague promise to give something to the museum in the future. If the museum accepts long-term loans from individuals, it may, because of the risks and the expense involved, wish to convince lenders that they should promise the objects loaned as future gifts.

The museum should offer the format of a letter of promised gift to future donors. Ideally the letter should be on the donor's letterhead, signed and notarized. It is not clear whether such letters will hold up in court. The owner might change, as well. Still, the letter might impress the donor and his or her heirs with the solemnity of the promise and act as a reminder when life changes—divorces, marriages, deaths—occur.

10. Proof of Purchase

Proof of purchase is handled differently at different museums. Laws, such as the Uniform Commercial Code, apply to title given by sale, but several gray areas exist that might cause problems if title is challenged.[35] Museum workers responsible for collection purchase transactions should become familiar with the iteration of the Uniform Commercial Code in the museum's state.

Well-conceived forms and thorough procedures that ensure that title is warranted by the seller to be free of liens or encumbrances will protect the interests of the museum. Similar to conditions on a deed of gift, a warranty of title might include:

- Name and address of vendor
- Name and address of museum
- Description of object
- Declaration of vendor's ownership or legal right to act for an owner
- Declaration that the object in question is authentic
- Declaration that the object in question has not been imported illegally or exported from the country of origin illegally
- Declaration that the object is not stolen or looted
- Notes on provenance, exhibition history, etc.
- Signature and date by vendor

The warranty may be preferred to a bill of sale because assurances about the object are given before the sale is finalized and title is transferred. One example of a sound process for purchase includes:

- Curatorial choice of object for purchase
- Receipt by the museum
- Internal discussion, director and collections staff
- Committee vote
- Warranty of title
- Payment and receipt

According to recent AAMD policies, museums are beginning to require, in addition to proof of purchase, extensive information on import status for classical objects coming to the United States. This includes country of origin and responses on customs form 7501. The Metropolitan Museum of Art, for instance, is requiring copies of that form and of the foreign export license as well as information about any other countries of export within the past five years. This tightening of documentation is a result of recent shifts in U.S.

responses to international claims and to lawsuits that have been brought against importing museums.

11. Partially Accessioned Objects

The process of accessioning includes the acquisition of the object as well as its recording. If there is evidence that an acquisition was completed, whether by written or oral contract, completing the accession entails simply recording the process. Add the transaction to the end of the year in which it was acquired, and follow the procedures in place for recording and tracking objects in the permanent collection. Museum workers may come across partially accessioned objects where the original value was low and there was hesitation to record the object because it was secondary, or because of a perceived intention to dispose of it in the future. Regardless of its value or desirability, if an object was acquired following the mode of acquisition for permanent collection in place at the date it entered the museum, it should be recorded. Even if it is to be deaccessioned, it must be tracked and a permanent record kept, so nothing is gained by not recording it.

12. Federally Owned Property

Allocation was a term used by the Works Progress Administration (WPA) of the Federal Government to indicate transfer of title for works created during that project. The Operating Procedures in the *Public Works of Art Program Bulletin*, March 26, 1934, indicates in Section 32, Part A, first paragraph: "For the purposes of this section 'allocated' shall mean transfer of title." However, a later part of the procedure notes a restriction regarding release from the responsibility of custody. The General Services Administration (GSA), in 2000, interpreted the manual to mean that allocated works were transfers of restricted title, and that the "receiving agency or institution received legal title to the works of art limited by the purpose stated in the allocation forms and by the regulations." Art made under the auspices of WPA programs is often allocated, but it may also be lent to an institution.

If a museum holds federal project works, however, it is vital to become familiar with GSA terms and uses. Carefully check all WPA objects for transfer of title, and contact the GSA, which currently oversees WPA works, if there is question of status.

13. Restricted Gifts

Registrars and collections caretakers prefer gifts with no restrictions. Restrictions may direct the way an object is stored and displayed, whether it may or may not be loaned or whether it might be deaccessioned. They must be clearly documented and followed.

Standard deeds of gift always carry language that gives the property to museums without restriction. Although perhaps more than 90 percent of gifts come without restriction, most museums have encountered a highly prized, important gift with definite guidelines for use, care or reproduction. In a brief survey, the Kelsey Museum of Archaeology reported taking no gifts with restrictions. Since the Kelsey is an archaeology museum it also has few problems with copyright, a legal form of restriction. Most museums have gifts with restrictions, and they also have objects covered by current copyright regulations.

Problems with restrictions are twofold. First, complying with restrictions already in place in collections demands a system that allows quick and easy determination of what restrictions might apply. A quick look at a database record, typically with a field tagged "restrictions," should yield the information needed. The database method, however, presumes that all objects for the collections are recorded and all records are complete. It is best to refer to original transaction papers when any question of a restriction arises. The classic cheat-sheet also works with restrictions, as it does with long-term loans.

Records should be checked for existing restrictions whenever the object is to be:

- Reproduced, internally or externally, academically or commercially
- Exhibited

- Loaned
- Conserved
- Deaccessioned

Second, curators and museum administrations should resist restrictions on new gifts. It is, of course, best to accept no restrictions if possible, copyright and artist's rights aside. If restrictions are demanded, the museum workers and committees who deal with gifts should decide on a case-by-case basis whether the acquisition is worth taking in light of the restriction. Negotiation by a careful and creative curator may resolve some of the problems. If something is taken with a restriction, it must be tracked carefully in the accession/object files, in databases and on cards. The museum worker's collection motto should be: Minimum restrictions, maximum vigilance.

Good and Bad Restrictions

One of the most difficult restrictions is also one of the most common: perpetual display. The difficulties can be compounded if not one object but a whole collection must be shown together and never removed from exhibition. The Barnes Foundation in Marion, Pa., has been one of the most visible and troubled examples of this type of restriction. Some museums, such as the Birmingham Museum of Art with its extensive Wedgwood collection, have made permanent exhibits into appealing parts of their overall displays. Problems with permanent exhibition become acute when it becomes difficult to meet conservation needs or when light begins to fade delicate colors in cloth and on paper.

Positive restrictions exist as well. One donor offered the complete nine-volume set of the 1842 John James Audubon *Birds of North America* if the museum promised that the volumes never be cut apart for individual exhibition of the prints. Since many sets have disappeared in favor of higher prices raised by individual prints, this restriction helped save a disappearing species.

14. Numbering Problems

Numbering museum objects has always presented a variety of problems. A unique number for each object is vital because it is the link between the object and its documentation. It must be clearly applied to objects and clearly noted on documents. Pages 45–46 discuss the general standard for assigning numbers to both accessioned and loaned objects. Problems, however, come in all shapes and forms.

If a museum had a careless registrar who paid little attention to the numbering system or, worse still, if the museum allowed anyone who "needed" a number to assign one, duplicate numbers inevitably resulted. In general, when two or more objects have the same number, it is best to keep the more completely established number with its object and assign a new number to the second object. The established number, which usually does belong to the more important object, is the number of the object that has been most often used, exhibited, published or conserved.

Assign the second object the next third number in its proper transaction in a three-part system or add it to the end of the year in a two-part system that includes year and object number. Since it is generally impossible to be certain that the number is changed wherever it might occur, always keep a record of the original number, the date it was changed, who changed it and why it was changed.

Sometimes whole systems are changed, from two-part to three-part, for example, or from sequential numbers to year numbers, usually from a nonstandard to a standard system. If such a change is made, it should be forward, never back. It is never easy to change numbers already in place. There is never enough staff time, and there are far too many chances for mistakes.

15. Lost in Inventory

The term "lost in inventory" describes a missing object that has been previously located but is not found when needed or when the next inventory is done. Even with good tracking systems in place, objects are often lost in inventory. A simple error—for example, putting the painting one bin over or the cup one shelf up—can make finding an object incredibly difficult.

Most lost objects are found at some point. One of the most famous instances is that of a bear-claw necklace that had been collected by Lewis and Clark and given to Harvard's Peabody Museum in 1941. It was mislabeled and lost for 62 years before it was discovered during an inventory by interns.[36]

Since it is rare that a museum can do a complete inventory, it is important to keep running location records and to update them with spot, room and complete inventories when possible. If something is lost, the last location should be checked, as well as logical places where it might be. In addition, the loans out, exhibition, conservation and photography lists should be reviewed. Lost objects almost always turn up.

There is no reason to deaccession an object or to remove an object record for something that is lost. In fact, it is important to keep the object in its current status. The object exists somewhere and belongs to the museum, and its documentation might yet connect it back to its home. Deaccessioning without disposition is simply an incomplete deaccession.

If museum workers conclude that an object is lost forever, they may file an insurance claim for "lost in inventory" if their insurance policies cover that particular loss. If the claim is paid, the insurance company will own the object if it is ever found, unless there is a "buy back" clause, and that provision should be noted in the object's file.

An example comes from Mark Janzen, registrar/collections manager of the Edwin A. Ulrich Museum of Art, Wichita State University, who writes:

In 1994 [museum staff] did a full inventory of the collection . . . and discovered that a number of objects were unaccounted for. After what I can only assume was a perfunctory search, they decided to deaccession the list of items as missing/lost/stolen.

Not surprisingly . . . some of them reappeared. None of the files had been discarded, so I was able to reaccession the objects and restore their files.[37]

Computers

Conundrum!

Do you let computers work for you or do you work for them?

Computer records should reflect the objects that have been in the collection since its beginning. Computers are also useful for tracking loans for exhibitions and objects received for study. Deleting records because they might "muddy" the data of current objects in the collection is not necessary. Rather, searches should be constructed to single out and report accurate information about the objects currently held by the museum.

16. Destructive Analysis

Knowing the composition, source and age of a piece can be crucial to its identification, care and treatment.[38] Sometimes, in order to gain this knowledge, destructive analysis must be performed. The application of scientific knowledge, techniques and technology in various disciplines has increased the frequency of destructive analysis. The types of objects subjected to different kinds of destructive analysis run the gamut from works of art to pieces of charcoal taken from a soil sample.

Destructive analysis normally involves taking a small, unobtrusive sample from an object; the size of the sample that must be sacrificed depends on the type of analysis being performed, the level of sensitivity required and the specific elements to be analyzed. Many techniques require samples measured in mere grams or milligrams, or even micrograms. Other advances have made destructive sampling unnecessary in certain circumstances. New, improved and/or more portable pieces of equipment may be available to investigate materials. The development of the environmental scanning electron microscope, for example, means that samples no longer need to be examined in a vacuum. Portable x-ray fluorescence equipment allows objects to be examined in place, making sampling unnecessary. If a destructive technique is required, conservation science has developed non-invasive methods, such as imaging, surface mapping and point analysis to examine and locate representative areas for the samples needed.

As always, it is best to have a formal policy. Requests for samples for destructive analysis may well come to the institution from outside researchers. In general, policies regarding destructive analysis should specify particular requirements, such as providing a description of the project and the knowledge to be gained from the analysis, justification for the use of samples from the collection and evidence that the technique being applied is appropriate to the question being asked and uses the least invasive methods and equipment available. Requests should be judged on their merit and whether the information to be gained will offset the loss.

17. Reaccessioning

"Reaccessioning" is probably not a word, but it clearly explains a situation that arises infrequently in museums in which an object that has been deaccessioned is, for some reason, brought back into the collection. Janice Klein notes an instance:

> *I worked at a museum that gave archaeological "duplicates" from the collections as a gift to members with a note that said something to the effect if you ever decide to get rid of this, please return it to the museum. Amazingly a number of those pieces came back, usually when the member died and their kids were cleaning out. The general practice at that time was to maintain the original accession number (which kept it in its historical context) and annotate the collections file accordingly.*[39]

If there is a reason to reaccession, maintaining the original number and annotating files is the simplest and best way to approach the process. It saves problems from complications that might arise from assigning two numbers and keeps the object history consistent.

18. Deaccessioning by Internal Transfer and Beyond

Museums sometimes, in their dark and devious pasts, transferred material internally when it was no longer wanted in the permanent collection. Since ownership did not change, it was reasoned, there was no need to deaccession. Some material was merely transferred from one curatorial division to another, with only nominal stewardship changing, so the reasoning in those cases is true. At other times, however, objects were transferred to educational, hands-on collections, loan collections or even special events departments.

In order to remain accountable, and to keep faith with the public trust, museums must always deaccession objects that will be given lesser care, even if they stay in the same institution. Putting an object in a permanent collection gives it a special status, and use by the institution in a less caring way should only happen when the object is taken out of the permanent collection, following due consideration and justification for such action, as outlined in museum policy. An object transferred to an educational collection is likely to be used up. Deaccession it before care changes. As a secondary precaution, establish a formal process for reporting collectionlike objects being disposed of by any department.

19. Ephemeral Objects

"Ephemeral object" is a term used to describe contemporary variable media objects that deteriorate or self-destruct. Some objects are meant to self-destruct, while others deteriorate because the base materials are not stable or because the workmanship was not a main concern of the artist. A museum should consider its liability and curatorial obligations carefully if it is offered an ephemeral object as a gift or if it desires to borrow one for an exhibition.

If the object is going to be a loan to the museum, it should be brought in under the usual loan agreement. Suzanne Quigley, a registrar who has dealt extensively with ephemeral objects, says that in the case of a loan the museum should "get the artist to sign a statement that he or she expects that the work will have deteriorated in whole or in part, that the museum will not insure it once it has been installed, and that he or she wants the remains returned or destroyed with evidence of destruction."[40] If the loan comes not from the artist but from a private lender, statements should be obtained from both regarding the care, insurance and disposition of the work.

If a museum acquires an ephemeral work, Quigley suggests that an interview with the artist is necessary so that artist's intention is known and documented. It is even possible that the artist will want specific types of documentation, which becomes the work of art once the original is gone. It is important to learn if the object is unique or part of a series, or if the museum will be allowed to recreate an object once it has deteriorated. She recommends a signed and dated cover certificate if this avenue is taken.

It is important to look into all aspects of this phenomenon if the museum has decided to use or acquire ephemeral works of art.

THE STRANGER WITHIN: MANAGING SUPPLEMENTAL COLLECTIONS

Holly Young

Most museums hold at least one kind of supplemental collection. Most of these collections have one thing in common: they assist the museum in achieving its mission in ways that would not be appropriate uses for objects from the permanent collection.

Since there is normally at least a superficial overlap between supplemental and permanent collections, these objects must be clearly marked and identifiable to the untrained eye, whether staff, volunteer or public. Not everyone who works in a museum is expert in all of its subject matter. Visitor services staff, for example, may be expert at interacting with the public, but not necessarily well versed in all of the material and objects presented by the institution.

Supplemental collection objects should be permanently marked in a manner that identifies them as property of the institution, but in a way that is distinctly different from labels used for the permanent collection. This will reinforce for staff and public that they are being allowed to use a special segment of the collection under special circumstances. Many supplemental collections objects, while they need to be identified and their use tracked, do not have an overabundance of information associated with them. A simple numbering and tracking system will do the job. For example, if the museum uses a typical three-part numbering system, supplemental collections could use a different system such as a unique, sequential alphanumeric designation, beginning with "ED-1" and continuing as needed. Marking methods should also be unlike those used for permanent collections objects in that they should be irreversible. Engraving or writing directly on a porous object with a marking pen will prevent the identification from being removed.

Keeping supplemental collections distinct from the permanent collection will save much time and effort on the part of those responsible for the permanent collection. Institutions usually exist for a long time, and institutional memory needs to be just as long. Individuals come and go, and no one can remember everything. The kinds of objects included as supplemental collections and the methods used to identify them must be documented and known by all staff members and made part of the training programs for new staff members.

The Fine Art of Choosing

History!

There was a time when it was common practice for museums to accept donations and decide after the fact whether or not an object would be accessioned. Some of the non-accessioned collection practices noted above indicate a willingness still to hold material and accession it at some future time if a curator so chooses. Lawrence Vail Coleman's *Manual for Small Museums* (1927) notes "if a useless object is weeded from an accession before cataloging, the only record needed is a memorandum in the accession book under Remarks." For several reasons—IRS regulations, the litigious nature of the late-20th-century United States, donor problems arising from misunderstandings—the practice of choosing objects for accession after donation is no longer commonplace. It is best for the curator to choose in advance and then let the donor know on the deed of gift which objects may go to a permanent collection and which may be used for education.

Types of Supplemental Collections

Fakes, forgeries, copies and other instances of questionable authorship

The terms "fake" and "forgery" have similar meanings and are most often used interchangeably. Both have the connotation of fraud and the intent to deceive on the part of the maker. For the purposes of this section, "fake" is used to describe objects intended as counterfeits in cases where the original objects were produced by anonymous makers, such as fake antiquities. "Forgery," on the other hand, refers to objects that are made to look like the work of a particular known artist with the intent to deceive a buyer, with or without a forged signature or maker's mark.[41]

It is traditional in art apprenticeships for students to make copies of recognized masterworks in order to learn and refine their techniques; artists also copy, revisit or rework their own creations. Acknowledged replicas are made for sale to collecting tourists. But fakes and forgeries are equally traditional. The studio system, in which apprentices paint backgrounds or specialize in creating particular effects, has long been used by artists who are much in demand to maximize their production. With group, student or creator copies, no intent to deceive exists, but copies must be clearly identified as such to prevent confusion. A museum which permits apprentice copies to be made of works in its collection should require a copyist to ensure distinctions from the original, such as making the copy larger or smaller and signing the copy with his or her own signature.

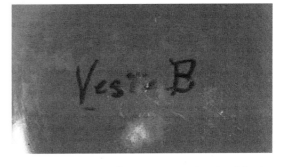

Pot bottoms, showing different signatures. Are they fakes or forgeries? Courtesy of the Pueblo Grande Museum, Phoenix.

Questionable authorship arises when doubt, for whatever reason, is cast upon the origin of a particular work. Signatures and makers' marks can be forged, so even the presence of these identifiers is not a guarantee of authenticity. Whether or not the work is signed, there may be some characteristic not in concert with the rest of the known body of work by a particular artist or craftsperson, which, along with a lack of documentation of the item's provenance, will raise questions. Museum staff members, collectors or other experts will evaluate such a work, hoping to attribute it to a particular artist. Whether declared genuine or not, lines of evidence and provenance must be objectively examined, and the reasoning behind the decision regarding the work's authenticity must be clearly documented. The conclusions of recognized experts can make a huge difference in the value of a piece, either positively or negatively. For this reason many museums decline to provide authentications for the public. A negative curatorial opinion does not make the piece less a work of artistic skill, but it does call into question the authenticity of a work, which generally devalues it. The converse is also true. While deaccessioning a piece determined to be inauthentic from the permanent collection is appropriate, keeping it in a supplemental collection may be prudent for many reasons, among them preventing the piece from resurfacing years later as a gift to the museum, to begin the cycle over again.

Known fakes, forgeries or copies still may have educational value to the museum. They can serve as a cautionary tale during employee or volunteer training, providing a graphic illustration of the reasons for museum policies regarding accepting objects for the museum. They can also be used for educational programs, as long as they are clearly identified as copies, fakes or forgeries by the instructor. They can be used as a discussion point for many different subjects, including the fascinating reasons why fakes or forgeries are created in the first place and their effects on people.

Example of a fake artifact; objects of this type are well known to have been forged. Courtesy of the Pueblo Grande Museum, Phoenix.

Records regarding decisions about the piece are kept permanently on file and are associated with the object through a uniquely identifiable numbering system. Works can be labeled with their deaccession number, if appropriate, and with a capsule description of the decision that has been reached regarding the object, such as "Copy of . . ." or "Forgery of (or by) . . . ." Labeling such pieces with tags, numbers or words that identify them as "Property of the XYZ Museum" is also appropriate.

Educational, Hands-On Collections

People love to touch the past. An object can make the story the museum tells come alive for the audience. Being able to touch an object can reinforce a story or idea, especially for those individuals who learn from touch or through experience.[42] Educational, hands-on collections are comprised of objects that have been identified for use or handling, normally in educational public programs. Each object has been carefully considered by a staff member or other knowledgeable individual, and the decision has been made that its value to the museum lies in its ability to educate through touch, with the understanding that "to use" can mean "to use up."

Education collections can be made up of lesser or redundant examples of a particular object, replicas or identified fakes or forgeries. Most, if not all, of them will closely resemble objects in the museum's permanent collection. They are normally kept in an area accessible to the public, such as classroom or exhibit areas, where they are identified and their use explained, either through signage or by a docent. In living history situations, the objects may be used in demonstrations. It is the responsibility of the institution and its representatives to make sure the public understands that there is a difference between the object they are being allowed to handle, or the one they see in use, and the objects in the museum's permanent collection.

Once again, labeling the pieces with a distinctive numbering system and/or property tags helps to reinforce this difference. It may also prevent their disappearance, which can occur even with staff and docent vigilance. If the public understands that the museum is tracking the items available for use, they may be less likely to wind up in a visitor's backpack or handbag.

Exhibition Materials

Sometimes, exhibits need to incorporate props or reproductions. This situation arises when the authentic item does not exist in the museum's collection and cannot be borrowed, or because the piece is too fragile or will not fit through the door to the exhibit gallery, or because of cultural sensitivities relating to the authentic object. For whatever reason, the exhibit curator or designer decides that a replica of the piece must be made to complete the story.

Very often, these props or replicas are clever reproductions of the original object with astounding verisimilitude. This is all very well and good during the run of the exhibition. But exhibits are changed, and people retire or move on to other jobs. Years later, the prop that was stuck on top of the shelving unit in storage is discovered and no one currently on staff knows that it is a replica, fabricated in-house, for the purposes of a long-ago and possibly long-forgotten exhibition. If the institution has less formal exhibits, especially ones not generated by staff activity, there is an additional source of confusion. This may be a particular problem for anthropological or history museums, which often go to great lengths to protect their reputation for authenticity.

Is this pottery paddle real? Was it actually used? Or created for exhibit in the early 1940s? Courtesy of the Pueblo Grande Museum, Phoenix.

Under these circumstances, while the museum may be justified in keeping the piece for its institutional archive, it is not appropriate for the permanent collection. The practice of unobtrusively labeling pieces with the exhibition title or number, reason for and date of manufacture and maker's name may prevent future confusion. Staff members will warmly compliment, even in absentia, a predecessor with such attention to detail. In addition, keeping good records on the museum's exhibits, including a list of replicas used along with the artifacts displayed and identified photographs of their installation, may save a great deal of work several decades from the present day.

Lending Collections and Study Collections

There are at least two different kinds of "lending collections." One is a collection put together for the express purpose of illustrating a particular principal, theory or type, and loaned to educational institutions for use in teaching students about this topic. These educational collections are generally assembled by an expert, sometimes not a museum staff member, and are usually held by museums whose mission encompasses the topic illustrated by the collection, and which therefore has a collection that contains similar objects. The items in the lending collection may be lesser or redundant examples or reproductions, or the exhibit may have been created outside of the museum without regard to the museum's collection. Closely related is the study collection, used by scholars or researchers, either at the institution or in their own place of study. These collections normally demonstrate the range of variability of a particular object. While these specimens may be largely undocumented, they still can provide an accurate portrait of this particular object type, and may assist in identifying or dating a particular piece. Sometimes, as with any actively used collection, keeping these materials well organized, and therefore useful, may be the biggest institutional headache they present. In addition, the overlap with a permanent collection is bound to be large. Having pieces permanently labeled and well inventoried, with records on their location and use, will keep the collection useful.

The second type of loan collection is generally art-oriented, and often found in museums embedded in larger institutions or even corporations. These are objects that are loaned out as "office art" to individuals or subsections of the larger institution. Since they are normally placed in less than ideal exhibit conditions, these are usually items of a lesser quality than the museum's permanent collection. Still, the overlap with the permanent collection may be significant, and the difference may only be apparent to an expert eye.

In both cases, these objects need to be tracked to prevent confusion and used in a manner that enhances the reputation of the museum that holds them. Rather than detracting from the museum's professionalism by having borrowers believe that the objects are from the museum's permanent collection, it must be made clear that these are objects that have been considered and selected specifically for such use, as opposed to curation in perpetuity. Using objects for educational purposes or for a social benefit, such as creating an environment where art and the pursuit of knowledge are part of everyday life and not restricted to special places, has long been a part of museum culture. In fact, some may argue that it is the most important reason for museums to exist.

Ephemera

"Ephemera" is hard to define because it is used in different ways by different types of collecting institutions. It normally refers to items manufactured specifically for use and disposal, mostly redundant printed items with limited time value, such as a playbill, invitation or menu, and also to three-dimensional objects, such as promotional items. Ephemera can also refer to objects or documents that have no relation to the activities of an institution or its collection.

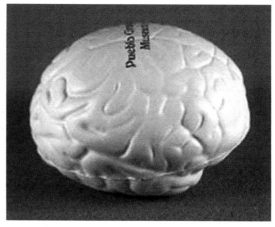

Promotional item—"donate your brain" squeeze toy. Courtesy of the Pueblo Grande Museum, Phoenix.

It is immediately apparent that one century's ephemera will turn into the next century's historical documentation; one museum's disposable ephemera collection is another museum's goldmine. The institution's mission, collecting policy and scope and its policy and procedures regarding the documentation of its own history dictate the distinction between ephemera and permanent collection. Each institution must define the distinction for itself, however, just as it must create its own mission statement. Only when the defining line has been drawn can museum staff be expected to adhere to it. Staff should be encouraged to refrain from accessioning or to deaccession existing collection items that fall on the side of ephemera and place them into more appropriate collections, such as the library or institutional archive.

Activities That May Result in Objects Not Part of the Collection Being at the Museum

Authentications and Appraisals

Museum staff members are trusted as experts by the public. Although some museums do not, many will open their doors to collectors to bring in their family treasures for an opinion. Some institutions have particular days or times set aside for this activity; others accept materials as temporary deposits for as long as it takes the curator or other knowledgeable staff member to study and form an opinion regarding the piece, its origins, manufacture, maker, condition and perhaps even value. These objects do not belong to the museum, even though the owner may intend to donate the items eventually. Holding such materials presents a risk management issue, and the institution must carefully document them as loans, recording and tracking them as they would any other loaned object, giving the pieces all the careful consideration they would give to their own permanent collection, and yet keeping them distinct from that collection.

The institution must have a policy on appraisal and authentication activities by staff, normally a part of the institution's ethics statement. If these activities are permitted, the museum must have liability insurance to cover possible claims by parties who believe they have been wronged by an undesirable declaration. As discussed earlier, the opinion of museum staff may have an appreciable positive or negative effect on the real or perceived value of the object, and the subsequent care that it receives from the owner.

In addition, there must be a designated staff member, preferably in the registration office, who handles incoming transactions for all objects similar to those collected by the museum. By carefully documenting the transaction and by storing materials properly while they are at the institution, the chances of loss or breakage are minimized, reducing the museum's liability.

Personal Property

Many museums forbid staff members to form personal collections in areas of interest to the museum, taking advantage of "insider knowledge," perhaps, or competing with the museum. Other museums may encourage collecting and connoisseurship in their staff, sometimes within the same collecting area as the museum. The museum's code of ethics must clarify the rights and responsibilities of both parties and provide guidelines for personal collecting, collecting area, how the collecting may be accomplished and what happens to the collection in the future. If the museum expects that the personal collection formed by a staff member will be donated by the staff member's estate or if the museum demands the right of first refusal, these expectations must be stated explicitly.

Sample Ethics Statement

Staff and volunteers of the XYZ Museum ensure that:

- Staff members do not deal in objects similar to those the museum collects.

- Staff members do not accept outside employment or consulting related to his or her field if there appears to be a conflict of interest, without appropriate disclosure.

- Staff members or volunteers do not use the museum premises for personal gain, or any object or item that is part of the museum collection, its property or items under the guardianship of the museum, except for official purposes sanctioned by the museum.

- Staff members do not develop personal collections—including speculative investing or dealing—in art, artifacts or specimens related to collection areas of the institution. Collecting is not pursued in competition with the museum and is appropriately and periodically disclosed.

Generally, museum staff members should be asked to supply an inventory of their personal collection, especially those pieces they have brought into the museum for use in their job or as office decoration. It is important for the institution to be aware of any objects on its premises that resemble those in their collections. This inventory should even extend to research resources, such as books, or tools, such as magnifiers. It is also important for the employee to understand whether or not personal property is covered by insurance while it is at the institution. For their own protection, staff members are encouraged to document their personal property and label it distinctively to make sure it is not mistaken for a collection object or a piece of the museum's property.

Use of the Museum as Storage by Another Entity

Although it is rare for a museum to have enough storage space for its own collections, it may occasionally agree to store materials for another institution or individual. If the museum has control over its own collection, objects stored there by another entity are easier to recognize. As recommended in the Personal Property section, the institution must receive an inventory of materials stored in its buildings or on its grounds that do not belong to it. A storage contract should be drafted to delineate the responsibilities of both parties. Many museums include the right to exhibit materials they agree to store in order to justify the investment of space and staff time in others' property. If possible, separate storage areas should be provided, to allow the organization or entity using the space freer access. If this is not possible, a staff member, designated coordinator of storage arrangements, can provide access to the storage for them. Under no circumstances should this entity receive keys to the museum facility.

Deaccessioning and Transfer

Best Practice!

Any object that is to be transferred from a permanent collection to a collection that is used, whether it be study, hands-on, library, exhibit or educational loan, should be first deaccessioned formally and then transferred internally. The intention of the museum is to move objects from a strict care situation to a more casually cared-for collection. If this transfer occurs without formal proceedings, according to museum policy, the museum does not uphold the public trust to care properly for its collections.

Ephemera

Ephemera inhabits a complex world. Collectible and attractive, ephemera has, at times, as in the Fluxus and other avant-garde movements, risen to the status of serious fine art. It is also the stuff of historical anecdotes and is found at the core of political collections. There are ephemera societies,[43] and almost all museums, libraries and archives contain ephemera. There are long and complicated documents with guidelines for cataloguing and preserving ephemera. Most museums, however, reach an uneasy solution: some ephemera is found in the museum's permanent collection, some in the institutional archives and some in the library's vertical files. Some is even kept in object files to support documentation of objects in a permanent collection.

Defining ephemera is difficult. Ephemeral objects are transient, primarily because of their materials, and they are widespread and broad in range. Ephemera includes materials we see and interact with every day: posters, tickets and ticket stubs, broadsides, pamphlets, bumper stickers, advertisements, sports give-aways, maps and brochures. Joan Reitz, in *ODLIS: The Online Dictionary of Library and Information*

Science, defines ephemeral materials as the "materials of everyday life, generally considered to have little or no permanent value, usually because they are produced in large quantities or in disposable formats."[44]

The way a museum deals with ephemera depends on the museum's mission and the type of its collections. The Margaret Woodbury Strong Museum places great value on ephemera and has a curatorial division dedicated to it. The Strong collects and accessions for the permanent collections a wide range of ephemera. Historical museums often accession posters, political memorabilia and stereopticon cards; art museums have posters in their permanent collections as well, and often collect ephemeral art. The Newark Museum and the New Jersey Historical Society have ephemeral collections in their libraries, archives and permanent collections. Decisions about disposition of ephemera are made ad hoc and depend on the specific type of object in question.

Libraries, including those associated with museums, often catalogue ephemeral collections only at the file level. The file level names the group but does not describe the individual objects that are contained in the group. Archival collections are often catalogued to the file level rather than object level, as well. Almost everything that enters the museum's permanent collection is catalogued on the object level. In order for a museum to deal effectively and consistently with ephemera, it must bring together the relevant staff and define the parameters of each collection. It is rare that a museum can declare that all ephemera will be accessioned into its permanent collection or will reside in its library or archives. It is usually an object-by-object decision that rests on good communication and is dependent on the tradition and format of the museum's various collections. When decisions are made, however, ephemera should be described and tracked as any other object in the collection in which it lands.

Traditional Lending Collections

Lending collections have a long history in American museums. Collections formally developed for use outside museums provide outreach services without putting permanent museum collections at risk. Traditional school lending programs have existed since the beginning of the twentieth century and can be found still in many museums ranging from the Oakland Museum, which lends suitcase natural science exhibitions, to the Natural History Museum of Los Angeles County, which has lent natural history specimens since the 1920s, to the Newark Museum, which continues to lend objects and small exhibitions from a special collection of 15,000 objects.

Newark's lending collection was begun in 1913 by John Cotton Dana, founding director of the Newark Museum and director of the Newark Public Library. It is comprehensive, and includes casts, economic products, objects depicting the lives and customs of people all over the world, models, natural history specimens, physical geography, textiles and toys. Early highlights were charts showing the processes of industry: cotton from the boll to cloth, lead smelting, leather making and use. In 1929 the museum lent 26,000 objects in one year, checking out objects to teachers and delivering them to schools.

Mr. Finley, at the wheel of the two-ton Graham Brothers truck that delivered objects to the Newark New Jersey Schools in 1928. Courtesy of the Newark Museum.

Non-Accessioned Collections

The Palmer Museum of Art at the Pennsylvania State University, University Park, Pennsylvania, has a group of objects they list as "University Collection." This collection consists of material useful for research but not of permanent collection quality. Objects receive numbers with the prefix UC; deeds of gift are not required, but donors are informed that the objects will not be in the museum's permanent collection. Although the UC collection receives the same standard of care that permanent collections do whenever possible, they are last on the list of priorities for conservation activities such as matting, framing and treatment. UC objects are tracked in the regular collections database.

—*Beverly Balger Sutley, registrar*

The Conner Prairie Living History Museum in Fishers, Indiana, has three collections: permanent, education resource and consumable material. The resource collection is tracked and numbered similarly to the permanent collection, but the consumables are not.

The educational resource collection makes up 95 percent of the collection and includes artifacts and more than 10,000 reproductions. The artifacts have the traditional year prefix, and the reproductions have a CPM (Conner Prairie Museum) prefix (e.g., CPM.4000). The numbers make it possible to distinguish between artifacts and reproductions. Both are entered into the collections management system, and both have individual catalogue cards, accession photos and document files.

Consumables are reproductions that are not expected to last more than two seasons. They include brooms, dust cloths, pencils, chalk, etc., and are not tracked in any way, not even a list for reference.

—*Lana Newhart-Kellen, registrar*

The National Building Museum in Washington, D.C., has a non-accessioned collection that is given "Unaccessioned" numbers. In the museum's database, the objects are tracked as "Unaccessioned 1," "Unaccessioned 2" and so on. The objects do come to the museum on regular deeds of gift.

—*Cecelia Gibson, exhibition registrar*

The North Carolina Division of State Historic Sites has categories of non-accessioned items. They are tracked in different ways, but they are all included on the deed of gift. On the deed of gift, each object's destination is noted so that the donor is fully aware of how their items are to be used. The collection of props has the prefix HSP and is tracked in the collections management database. These are items that are used in displays but may be reproductions. There are also a teaching collection that sites may use for demonstration purposes and a library research collection. These do not get numbers, nor are they tracked in the database.

—*Elizabeth Sumner, registrar*

The Minneapolis Institute of Arts has several types of non-accessioned objects in use by the museum. They always require a deed of gift for the transfer of objects. One category, which includes study items, props for the period rooms and didactic materials like tools to make something else, is called "Accepted, Not Accessioned"; these objects live forever associated with the loan numbers that were assigned when they entered the museum. The staff believes that it lessens problems to avoid multiple numbering schemes. The museum does keep track of the locations of non-accessioned materials in general, the most notable exception being the objects the education department uses as hands-on props for family day activities. Those objects are treated as consumables.

—*Leslie Ory Lewellen,*
assistant registrar for acquisitions

The Lakeview Museum of Arts and Sciences in Peoria, Illinois, has two separate categories for its reference collection. One, Program Support, contains inferior quality objects and props. Those pieces, approved by the Collections Committee, are accessioned with a different numbering system beginning with PS, such as PS2005.1 (the first program support item of 2005). The donor is informed that the item is going into the Program Support collection, and the transaction is completed by deed of gift.

The second reference collection belongs to a School Loan program. The objects in that collection are used in outreach programs and are meant to be handled. They are not accessioned and a staff person in the education department keeps track of them. The collections department is not involved with those objects.

—*Laura Gharst, collections manager*

The Mesa Southwest Museum in Mesa, Arizona, has reference collections that are often broader in scope than the museum's mission but are used in the paleontology and archaeology labs for comparative purposes. These objects are accessioned, numbered, entered into the collections database as any other accessioned material, tracked by general location and stored in the labs with a lower level of security than that given to permanent accessioned collections. A deed of gift is signed for each donation.

The museum also has a hands-on, meant-to-deteriorate, education collection that is not accessioned. If these are donated items, the museum asks the donor to sign a regular deed of gift marked "nonaccessioned objects." These deeds are kept in a special collections file in case one day in the future a curator decides that any of them are worthy of being accessioned. This has happened several times. In addition, collections personnel also keep receipts for purchased items that are put into the educational collections or that are designated for use as exhibit props. These objects are not tracked, but each is marked with ED or EX so that they can be identified.

Contemporary reproductions, still commonly for sale, are also marked ED or EX and turned over to the appropriate department.

—*Paula Liken, museum registrar*

The educational loan collection is completely separate from the museum's permanent art and science collections. It is administered through the education department, which develops and maintains its own exhibitions. In times past it reported to the director. The objects receive "X" numbers, which otherwise mimic the accession numbers of the permanent collection, i.e., X2000.5.1. The collection is catalogued in the museum's collection database, though circulation is handled separately. It has remained a major component of the museum's educational programming for almost a century.

University Loan Collections

Universities have complex collection issues; lending and renting art to students, professors and administrative offices is interwoven with differentiating departmental and personal collections from university museum collections. There have been art lending programs for students in universities, and some museums, such as the Allen Art Museum at Oberlin College, still maintain a rental collection for students. In that program each student is allowed two works of art each semester. Other programs for students, those at Dartmouth College and Smith College, for example, have been discontinued.

University museums always have pressure to lend to administrative offices and to conserve the historical portraits of past administrators. Smith College had, at one time, a rental collection from which students could borrow, loan collections that employees could use both at home and at work and a college collection of portraits that graced offices and public areas. During the late 1990s the rental collection, primarily unaccessioned material of low value, was dismantled; students were not interested and the drain on staff time was no longer justifiable. Most unaccessioned objects were, after curatorial review, discarded. The loan collection has been slowly shut down, and works that were part of it either deaccessioned or returned to the permanent collection. Lending was suspended, and material that was in offices was either recalled or returned. College portraits, however, remain a responsibility of the museum.

Who is Responsible for What?

Conundrum!

Collections in colleges and universities grow slowly and informally. Through such avenues as gifts to departments, commissioned portraits of major figures and works by artists-in-residence, these collections can be scattered across campus. Museums are sometimes formed to hold collections of art, archaeology or history important to the greater institution. In order to remain accountable for its collections, a university must make clear decisions about stewardship of all collections. How it does this will depend on the type and extent of its holdings, the types of museums (if any) that it has formed and the influence of staff of the university's museums, libraries and risk management offices. The university may make its art museum steward of all art on campus, it may hire a special staff to oversee art objects or it may assign them to the special collection department of its library. It is most important to have a designated department responsible for care and oversight; that department can lobby for funds for care and conservation and make decisions about the judicious use of collections.

Art Rental Programs

There are art management programs that rent the work of local artists to homes and businesses; the Seattle Art Museum, Portland Art Museum and Northwest Museum of Arts and Culture (MAC), for example, have such programs.

The Art at Work program at the MAC involves a collection completely separate from the permanent and custodial collections that are central to the museum. Founded in the early 1990s, Art at Work is based on similar programs at the

Portland (Oregon) Art Museum and the Seattle Art Museum. Its mission is to provide a central venue for placing the work of contemporary local and regional artists:

The Sales and Rental Program of the Northwest Museum of Arts and Culture provides our community with access to contemporary art of enduring quality through a program that fosters collaboration, exposure, and financial support for regional artists and the Museum.

The manager of the program keeps a gallery full of works available for rental or purchase through constant contact with artists. The museum offers these works for rent or sale and sends 60 percent of revenue to the artist, keeping 40 percent for maintenance of the program. Works are rented for a three-month term and can be renewed, purchased or returned to the museum at the end of the period. The museum transports, installs and maintains the works as part of the transaction.

The program provides a valuable service to artists and helps businesses and private patrons bring art into their offices and homes. The old practice of providing art from the permanent collection for offices has dwindled in the museum world—though it still exists within government offices and in university settings—and this type of program encourages a positive interaction rather than a stewardship dilemma caused by requests from the community.

The MAC's museum van. Courtesy of the Northwest Museum of Arts and Culture.

Notes

1. Charles Hummel, "The Role of the Registrar in the Museum's Web," in *New Museum Registration Methods,* edited by Rebecca A. Buck and Jean Allman Gilmore (Washington, DC: American Association of Museums, 1998), xvi.

2. Judith L. Teichman, "In Support of a Legislative Solution to the Problems of Objects of Uncertain Status in Museum Collections," in *Legal Problems in Museum Administration* (n.p.: ALI-ABA, 1983), 298.

3. Ibid.

4. Judith L. Teichman, "Museum Collections Care Problems and California's 'Old Loan Legislation.'" *COMM/ENT: Hastings Communications and Entertainment Law Journal* 12: 3 (Spring 1990), 452.

5. Deardorff's Glossary of International Economics, http://www-personal.umich.edu/-alandear/glossary/ (accessed Feb. 22, 2007).

6. The term "permanent loan" was used in the profession some years ago. Loans by definition are temporary and therefore it is unclear what the parties had in mind when the arrangements for permanent loans were made. Often a review of the museum's records may indicate that a gift was actually intended or completed. If title to the object still rests with the lender, however, then permanently loaned objects should be treated as loans of unlimited duration.

7. It is important to note that "old loans" do not include undocumented objects found in the museum's collections, so-called FICs. These FICs lack any documentation as to how they were acquired by the museum.

8. This situation may be getting worse as many museums are forced to downsize due to budgetary constraints.

9. L. K. Wise, "Old Loans: A Collections Management Problem," *Legal Problems of Museum Administration* (Philadelphia: ALI-ABA, 1990), 44; Agnès Tabah, "The Practicalities of Resolving 'Old' Loans: Guidelines for Museums," *Legal Problems of Museum Administration* (Chicago:

ALI-ABA, 1992), 317; and Ildiko DeAngelis, "Old Loans: Laches to the Rescue?" *Legal Problems of Museum Administration* (Chicago: ALI-ABA, 1992), 202.

10. For a full discussion of the legal problems of "unclaimed loans" and possible solutions, see Marie Malaro, "Unclaimed Loans," *A Legal Primer in Managing Museum Collections* 2nd ed. (Washington, DC: Smithsonian Institution Press, 1998): chapter 7, 284–311.

11. In 1997 there were only 23 states with such laws in place. Around that time, the Mid-Atlantic Association of Museums Registrars Committee (RC-MAAM) formed an Old Loan Task Force charged with drafting model legislation for that region. RC-MAAM widely circulated the model which the task force developed to gather support for legislative efforts in states lacking old loan laws. See "Model Museum Unclaimed Property Law," Fig VII.2 in Malaro, *Legal Primer*, 300–303.

12. In the one reported court decision from the District of Columbia involving an old loan, the court held that the paintings on loan to the museum for decades had to be returned to the lender's heirs. *In re Therese McCagg*, 450 A.2d 414 (D.C. cir. 1982). The court noted that the museum had failed in that case to make a reasonable effort to notify the lender's heirs and refused to find that the loan had expired at the lender's death. However, the court noted in a footnote that if the lenders cannot be located by the museum after reasonable efforts, notice to the lenders or heirs by publication in a newspaper may be legally sufficient. Notice by publication was not directly at issue in the case. *Id.* at 418.

13. In addition to the statute of limitations approach, the legal doctrines of adverse possession and laches may help a museum successfully defend a case brought by a long overdue lender for return of an old loan. The usefulness of these doctrines is discussed in Malaro, *Legal Primer,* 296–97; and DeAngelis, "Old Loans," 202. Actions taken by the museum under the statute of limitations approach discussed in this

chapter will also support these alternate defenses and are not separately addressed here.

14. Tabah, "Practicalities," 330–31.

15. See "Resolving Unclaimed Loans Using the Internet: Resources and Case Studies," by Graduate Students and Faculty of the Museum Studies Program, the George Washington University, in *Legal Problems of Museum Administration* (Washington, DC: ALI-ABA, 2002), 208–221.

16. Ibid.

17. Agnès Tabah, "Practical Guidelines in Resolving Old Loans: Guidelines for Museums" in Malaro, *Legal Primer,* pp. 304—311.

18. California Civil Code, sec. 1899.10(b)

19. For example, see the old loan statutes of California, Wyoming, Missouri and Kansas.

20. For example, see the old loan statutes of Indiana, Missouri and South Carolina.

21. Agnès Tabah, "Old Loans: State Legislative Solutions," unpublished research paper, December 4, 1991, prepared for the George Washington University Museum Studies Program course on Collections Management: Legal and Ethical Issues. A national survey of the use of old loan laws by museums is overdue.

22. Ibid.

23. See Patricia Nauert, "Glossary," in Dorothy M. Dudley and Irma Bezold Wilkinson, *Museum Registration Methods,* 3rd ed. (Washington, DC: American Association of Museums, 1979), 412.

24. Mary H. Lawson, "How One Collection Is Getting Its Groove Back: Revitalizing the National Postal Museum's Exhibit and Master and Reference Collection of U. S. Stamps," *EnRoute,* 1998. www.postalmuseum.si.edu/resources/6a2t_usstampproject.html (accessed, Feb. 9, 2007).

25. Ildiko DeAngelis, "Old Loans and Found in Collection," paper presentation at the American Association of Museums Annual Meeting, Indianapolis, Indiana. May 2005.

26. Malaro, *Legal Primer,* 356–359

27. Ildiko DeAngelis and Jeanne Benas, pers. comm., 2005.

28. Don Moser, "Offerings at the Wall,"

Smithsonian Magazine 26:2 (May 1995) 54.

29. Thanks to Katie Speckart for her diligent Internet searching.

30. See also the American Association of Museums' website (www.aam-us.org), for current information.

31. Douglas F. Browne, Esq., pers. comm., 2005.

32. "Agreement for Purchase and Sale of the William Bradford Cup and For Its Subsequent Disposition and Display," between the Smithsonian Institution National Museum of American History and The Pilgrim Society, March 8, 1985.

33. Ibid.

34. http://www.wsba.org/media/publications/pamphlets/marriage.htm (accessed Feb. 9, 2007).

35. Malaro, *Legal Primer,* 65–72.

36. http://www.csmonitor.com/2004/0831/p18s02-hfks.html (accessed Feb. 9, 2007).

37. RC-AAM listserv, September 2005

38. We thank Holly Young for her contribution to this section.

39. RC-AAM listserv, September 2005.

40. Suzanne Quigley, Art and Artifact Services, New York, pers. comm., 2005.

41. For a discussion of this topic by several different authors, including the effects of highly influential fakes, see Mark Jones, ed. *Fake? The Art of Deception* (Berkeley and Los Angeles: University of California Press, 1990).

42. For examples, see Howard Gardner, *Frames of Mind: The Theory of Multiple Intelligences* (New York: Basic Books, 1983); and *Intelligence Reframed: Multiple Intelligences for the 21st Century* (New York: Basic Books, 1999).

43. http://www.ephemerasociety.org/news/newsreport23.html (accessed 2/9/07)

44. http://www.slais.ubc.ca/courses/libr513/03-04-wt1/projects/Ephemera.ppt (accessed Mar. 22, 2007).

3: Guidelines, Policies and Procedures

In addition to resolving old collection problems, museums must establish systems and procedures to prevent future problems. There are three components to a sound collection system:

- Collecting guidelines
- Collection management policy
- Collection procedures

Together, these components provide clear control of the collection. Material is accepted into the collection on the basis of need and planned collection growth. Decisions regarding each transaction are clear, necessary legal transactions occur and the object(s), once in the collection, are treated systematically. The result of following these guidelines, policies and procedures should be no found-in-collection objects, no old loans and no partially accessioned objects in the future. Collection problems can be limited to occasional human error.

JUST SAY NO!

A donor appears at the door of a regional historical museum, offering a large collection of Chinese tourist-trade objects he picked up while in China, a local wedding gown that is fifty years old and a basket made by a local Native American tribe two hundred years ago.

Without collecting guidelines, museum staff will make a personal response to this donor, accepting as much as believed necessary to get the one object (the basket) that would enhance the collection. Having collecting guidelines in place enables museum staff to tell the donor what can and cannot be accepted and why. It does not make the human interaction simple, but such a document makes the museum's best interests more attainable.

Unless there is a collections management policy in place, staff may put aside the less desirable parts of the acquisition (Chinese objects, dress) and accession only the basket. A policy requires explanations to and approvals from the powers that be and will necessitate accessioning everything. Knowing the requirements that lie ahead may cause museum workers to think twice before accepting the entire offering. If not, the museum will be stuck with unusable materials in storage until future staff undertake a deaccession campaign.

If the entire lot is accessioned, museum workers can simply assign numbers to the objects and stash the undesirable ones in the attic. The board will never know. The basket will be catalogued, photographed and prepared for exhibition; the other objects will never see the light of day. Ethical adherence to collection procedures and control, however, demands that all of the objects be documented properly and stored as safely as possible.

Taking an entire collection to get the one or two objects the museum really needs puts the museum in a complicated and costly situation. The future, as unwanted objects accumulate, becomes darker with each new group. All of the objects that come in must be processed, which, if they are handled properly, takes staff time. Volunteer time is to be cherished and used wisely; staff time is costly and must be used efficiently.

The objects must be stored, and the storage space, since it is to be of museum quality, must be climate controlled and secure. HVAC systems and security personnel's salaries cost a great deal of money. The objects will not be stored for a week or a year but potentially forever. The decision to accept unwanted Chinese objects and a wedding dress ultimately costs not just the initial staff time but also an escalating amount per year for storage and overhead. And there are also the costs of inventories, documentation, conservation and the long slow march of the deaccession process.

History!

It has come to be recognized that a collection should not be made haphazard, but should have some definite purpose, and the specimens of which it is composed be parts of a connected and consistent whole.

—F. A. Lucas, "The Evolution of Museums," 1908

Collection Planning

Control of collections has traditionally begun when objects enter the collection. The American Association of Museums has, however, developed collecting guideline templates that museums can use to guide consideration of and plan for collection additions and deaccessions. It is likely that firm collecting guidelines will become a requirement for AAM accreditation. Information on collections planning may be found in *The AAM Guide to Collections Planning* by James B. Gardner and Elizabeth B. Merritt.

A sound collections plan includes an intellectual framework that encompasses the museum's mission and collecting. It begins by describing the history and current composition of the collections, pointing out strengths, weaknesses and gaps. It then molds the visions of various curators, along with that strong dose of mission and history, into an institutional vision that encourages the curators to place the disparate demands of their particular collections into perspective with the broader needs of the institution as a whole.

The goal of the planning phase is to set priorities, develop strategies for collecting and delineate criteria for acquisition and deaccessioning. Museum workers identify desired collections, describing types of collections and specific objects that are needed. The museum should be able to move from passive to active collecting with planning in place; at the very least, it should be able to say yes or no with certainty and with the power of its governing board behind it when gifts are offered.

History!

So, it would be possible to make an exhibition of great popular interest, not one object of which should be publicly exhibited. The two objects most frequently asked for in the National Museum were Guiteau's skeleton and the books made of human skin.

—F. A. Lucas, "The Evolution of Museums," 1908

The result of planning, acquiring only relevant collections that can be used and cared for both intellectually and physically, also builds morale. Collections staff are often overwhelmed with current tasks. If backlogs exist or build, frustration and inability to perform increase as staff morale drops. Accountability starts with judicious acquisition.

Collection Control

There are many important reasons for a museum to control its collections. Museums must be accountable in order to keep legal status, manage risk and build and maintain public trust. Accountability includes knowing every object in a collection, including its exact legal status, location, condition and history, how it is researched and how it is to be stored or exhibited.

In 2005 AAM updated its accreditation guidelines and included a category among the characteristics of an accreditable museum not found in the 1995 version: public trust and accountability. The first point in the category states that "the museum is a good steward of its resources held in the public trust." The section on collections stewardship was also expanded in 2005 to include the following:

- The museum owns, exhibits or uses collections that are appropriate to its mission.

- The museum legally, ethically and effectively manages, documents, cares for and uses the collections.

- The museum's collections-related research is conducted according to appropriate scholarly standards.

- The museum strategically plans for the use and development of its collections.

- Guided by its mission, the museum provides public access to its collections while ensuring their preservation.

—AAM checklist, Characteristics of an Accreditable Museum, 2005

Accountability looms large in everyone's mind when accreditation or reaccreditation is underway, or when a self-study is undertaken to improve some part of a museum's operation. It comes to mind whenever a grant application is being written and a case made to show the professional status of the organization. It comes to a collection manager or curator's attention when a loan is found to be missing and the lender is standing there waiting to see his or her objects. It comes to the public's attention when there is a serious problem with a museum's use or care of collection. Lack of control forms the basis of a million sticky situations.

The practical reasons to control a collection are simpler. Museum workers must be able to find an object needed for loan or exhibition. They must know what credit line to put on a label when it is on display. They must answer questions from scholars and the general public and produce objects for programs and publications. They must be able to answer a donor's or lender's question regarding objects in the collection. In order to conserve objects effectively, museum workers must know how they were treated in the past.

Everything good in a museum's program flows from collection control, which, in turn, flows from sound accessioning and cataloguing procedures and from complete periodic inventories. Here is a checklist of things that must be done if a museum is to control its collections:

- All objects in the museum's permanent collection are completely accessioned.

- All accessioned works have their accession numbers soundly attached to them.

- All accessioned works are catalogued, preferably in a computer database.

- All accessioned works have photographs.

- Locations of all collection objects are recorded and current.

- The museum has clear guidelines for deciding whether an object should be accessioned as:

  Ephemera

  Rare books

  Study collections

- The museum has clear guidelines for identifying objects that are not accessioned, including:

  Short-term loans

  Long-term loans

  Gifts and purchases on approval

  Library material

  Archival material

  Educational, hands-on collections

  Lending collections

  Exhibition props

  Object accessories

  Reproductions, fakes, forgeries

  Decorations for special events

  Office art, either personal or institution-owned

- Non-accessioned objects mixed with collection objects are clearly marked.

- Catalogue information for non-accessioned objects is also on cards, or in a database.

Achieving needed control is a product of well-conceived policies and clear procedures that can be followed by an adequate number of trained staff. To be a professional organization a museum must develop the policies and acquire the necessary staff.

POLICIES AND PROCEDURES

As noted above, three sets of policies and procedures work together to establish collection control and accountability:

- Collecting guidelines

- Collection management policy

- Collection procedures

These tools all derive from the mission of the museum.

Collection Management Policies

Museums must have sound collection management policies. Once the collecting guidelines have been used to determine that an object should be acquired for the permanent collection, the collections management policy will guide the museum worker through the legal and ethical dilemmas of acquisition. Further policies will give guidance on loans, collection care, access, storage and deaccession.

In 2006, the American Association of Museums published *Things Great and Small: Collections Management Policies* by John Simmons to help museums devise effective collection management policies, offering samples and outlining current standards of practice.

Policies for the following core functions provide the foundation of collections control:

- Acquisitions

- Deaccessions

- Loans in

- Loans out

- Access to collections

A collections care component that sets out guidelines for collections care, documentation, storage control, insurance, security and conservation issues is also valuable.

Policies are usually shaped according to samples from publications and from other museums, by the registrar or a collections administrator, and then discussed and refined in collaboration with curatorial and collections management staff. Once thoroughly reviewed by staff, the director presents the policies to the board of trustees for approval. Collection management policies should reflect current professional standards of practice as well as the traditions and historical practices of the individual museum; they should be reviewed and updated at regular intervals.

Collection Procedures

In order to control collections intellectually and physically, the descriptions and systems used to access them must be clear, simple and consistent. Discussions of procedures for basic museum functions can be found in *The New Museum Registration Methods* by Rebecca Buck and Jean Gilmore (1998). Museums use various systems, but evolved practices should be followed as closely as possible. Systems are also defined for the new museum to adopt; new museums, especially those run by volunteers, should avoid trying to reinvent systems. If they start with simple guidelines and follow them as closely as possible, future problems will be averted.

With procedures for accessioning, lending and borrowing, deaccessioning, interdepartmental activities, proper storage and photography, procedures manuals can grow to enormous size. To avoid found-in-collection objects and old loans, however, following a few basic procedures may make the difference between future problems and a smoothly functioning museum.

Initial Recording

When an object enters a museum, the museum establishes a relationship with the owner of that object. The relationship has serious responsibilities, and because of this the relationship must be clear. If an object is intended as a gift, the museum does not own the object until title transfers upon completion of a gift transaction. Transfer of title results from a letter of intent, a letter of acknowledgment and physical possession of the object or, more simply, from a deed of gift signed by both parties and physical possession of the object. The museum does not gain title to a potential purchase until payment is made. The museum never gains title to a loan on its premises unless the lender converts it to a gift or the museum, when it is no longer able to find the lender, undertakes a legal process to claim the loan as its own.

The initial processing of an object into a museum is the one sure path toward keeping the status of objects clear. It should be similar for all objects coming into the museum, whether they be loans for short- or long-term exhibition, gifts and purchases on approval or objects for study or examination. All objects not owned and already accessioned and anything that looks like an object that might be stored with the museum's collection should be processed in the same manner.[1] Initial processing should include a numbering scheme that differs from permanent collection sequences. Permanent numbers are generally tripartite and include:

Year.Accession transaction. Object.

For example, the first permanent collection transaction of the year 2007:

2007.1.1 Painting

The object number may be followed by letters or numbers indicating part/whole or set relationships as necessary:[2]

2007.1.2a,b	Pair of shoes
2007.1.3a–d	Chest of drawers with three removable drawers
2007.1.4.1–10	Portfolio of photographs

The second transaction of 2007:

| 2007.2 | Painting |

Part/whole

Conundrum!

How do you decide if a tea set is a part/whole relationship or a set?

It is always best to ask the expert in the field, the curator of the collection involved. A knowledgeable curator will know, for example, if a tea set was purchased as a whole or whether it was assembled from several individual purchases. He or she will know if a costume is really a whole, or made up of parts that are of different origins. If such an expert is not available, research must be done.

In this case, with only one object in the accession, the third part of the number is unnecessary. In fact, more information is given by the absence of the number than would be by its presence; it tells the person reading the number that there is only one object in the accession.

The numbering system for objects not owned by the museum may be called temporary deposit, holding or temporary receipt. It often includes a recognizable prefix (T, TR, etc.) and is usually reversed from the permanent collection sequence:

Transaction.Year.Object

The TR (temporary receipt number), given to the first group of objects before ownership transferred to the museum, might appear as follows:

TR1.2007.1	Painting
TR1.2007.2a,b	Pair of shoes
TR1.2007.3a–d	Chest of drawers with three removable drawers
TR1.2007.4.1–10	Portfolio of photographs

The second transaction would then begin TR2.2007. The system to record temporary numbers should be as simple as possible. Pages in a three-ring notebook or a bound ledger, or entries in a computerized database should include the following information, together on one line:

TR number assigned

Date

Department or staff member involved

Type of transaction (loan, gift on approval, etc.)

Number of objects

For example, temporary receipts for 2007:
TR1.2007   1/3/2007   Dec Arts/Art
         Smith gift on approval   5 vases
TR2.2007   1/6/2007   Art
         Loan for Portrait exhibition 1 painting

This type of ledger, similar to the accession ledger of old, should be used to avoid assigning numbers more than once.

Year

Conundrum!

Is it necessary to use all four digits of the year in numbering systems?

Absolutely! Most museums did not do this during the 1900s and now a batch of ambiguous numbers (9.200, 85.164.1, etc.) in use must be clarified. In one museum, when the first one hundred years had rolled by in 1973, the first number system, using 73 for 1873, became obsolete and an equally difficult system, using 173 to stand for 1973, was substituted. It is best to use all four year numbers, if possible. It is also wise to avoid changing past numbers. Adopting a four-digit pattern now will provide numbers distinct from earlier assignments when the museum's centenary occurs. Simplicity and clarity rule.

Once the transaction number is assigned, the objects can be processed separately. A condition report for each object, with a complete description and measurements, should be produced. The object should be photographed if possible. An inexpensive digital camera can be used for this purpose; a photograph is much more definitive than the subjective description and should be used whenever possible to identify the object and to help record its condition.

If the museum uses a computerized collection database, information about the transaction and each object in it should be entered and should remain permanently. Although some museum workers like to remove records of objects that are returned or deaccessioned, cards should never be removed from a hard copy file and records should stay in a database. An effective database will allow the worker to devise a search that will find only those objects desired.

The object should be tagged with an acid-free tag—not indelibly marked as the museum would mark its own permanent collection—and needed storage mounts should be applied. The object should be put in storage or on exhibition, according to its intended use, and the location should be noted.

The receipt issued to the owner should have at least three copies: one for the notebook containing the list of temporary holdings, one for the owner and one for the working file (loan, exhibition, approval, etc.). When objects leave the museum, an outgoing receipt is issued, and the incoming receipt should be annotated to indicate that the transaction is closed. A year-end review of all transactions for the year will indicate what is left in the museum, and records should be updated as needed.

An incoming receipt must identify owner, address, object description and the exact nature of the transaction. This information is essential to identify, process or return the objects involved (see appendix C).

Object Movement

Another invaluable tool to avoid problems with stray objects is a sound system to maintain current locations of all objects.

Museums note locations either on a card system or in a computer database, including the date, location and initials of the person recording it. It is important that changes in location be logged and updated on either the card or in the database. This process, too, should be as simple and straightforward as possible. It should apply to all temporary and permanent holdings in the museum.

Accession/Catalogue

Conundrum!

What is the difference between an accession number and a catalogue number?

A catalogue number is descriptive, while an accession number is a control number that connects the object to its documentation. Most non-science museums use only accession numbers.

If the museum is very fortunate, it will record current locations in a computer database, and networked computers will be available in storage areas to update movements as they happen. More often, a logbook or a paper system is completed at the time of the move and the information later transferred to a computer or to the card system. In this case, it is absolutely necessary to update records on a regular basis, in order to maintain control of the collection.

Inventories are often talked of, but not often completed. It is important for a museum to do a base inventory that can be used for future checks and can be amended as new objects come to the museum. If it is not possible to complete a base inventory, an inventory can be built piecemeal, though the lack of information for many objects can be frustrating and make it difficult to resolve problems. The preferred inventory is a complete inventory justified against object documentation. It should be repeated on a regular basis, and spot checks should be done randomly between complete inventories.

Acquisition, Loan, Deaccession

The procedures for acquisitions, loans and deaccessions have been described in great detail in *New Museum Registration Methods* and are discussed at length by professional committees in their literature, at conferences and in museum study courses. The important points to remember are that the processes must be executed in accordance with the history, tradition and collection management policies of each museum, and that a clear written record for each is essential.

Loan procedures must be precise and follow-up diligent in order to avoid future old loans. Loan agreements should be in writing and should be executed before any object is taken into the custody of the museum. The loan agreement should contain as much contact information as possible: lender's name, address, phone, e-mail. The loan material must be processed as all incoming material that is not already the property of the

museum is processed. A clause that states that the owner must contact the museum if there is a change of address or if ownership changes is also important (see appendix C).

Florida's museum-specific old loan legislation requires, as do the statutes in many states where old loan legislation has passed, that a museum adhere to a procedure to prevent old loans from happening in the future. It lists a museum's responsibilities, providing a useful guideline for museums everywhere, not just in Florida:

265.565 3   Obligations of Museums to Lenders

(a) For property loaned to a museum after the effective date of this act, the museum shall:

1. Make and retain a written record containing, at a minimum, the lender's name, address and telephone number, a description of the property loaned in sufficient detail for clear identification, including a description of the general condition of the property at the time of the loan, the beginning date of the loan and the expiration date of the loan.

2. Provide the lender with a signed receipt or loan agreement containing, at a minimum, the record set forth in subparagraph 1.

3. Inform the lender of the existence of the provisions of this act and provide the lender with a copy of the provisions of this act upon the lender's request.

(b) Regardless of the date of a loan of property, the museum shall:

1. Update its records if a lender informs the museum of a change of address or change in ownership of property loaned, or if the lender and museum negotiate a change in the duration of the loan.

2. Inform the lender of the existence of the provisions of this act when renewing or updating the records of an existing loan and provide the lender with a copy of the provisions of this act upon the lender's request.

(c) A museum shall give a lender prompt notice of any known injury to or loss of property on loan.

The above provisions give minimum standards for basic loan registration. To ease the task of tracking, loans may be numbered differently from accessions. A museum might keep the temporary number, as above, or it may devise a loan numbering system. Some museums use loan numbers for long-term loans but not for short-term or exhibition loans. The museum's procedures should follow the loan policy, and be written and accessible to staff.

The L (loan–in) number given to the first group of objects might be as follows:

L1.2007.1	Painting
L1.2007.2a,b	Pair of shoes
L1.2007.3a–d	Chest of drawers with three removable drawers
L1.2007.4.1–10	Portfolio of photographs

TR to Loan

Conundrum!

When do you change a TR to an L?
Some museums keep a TR (temporary receipt) number as the active number and do not change to an L (loan) number, but this might become confusing if there is a backlog in accessioning. L numbers may be assigned as soon as objects arrive at the museum, or TR numbers may apply to short term exhibition loans and L numbers only to loans that are long term, i.e., at least one year.

Other helpful guidelines include making loans for no longer than one year's duration and renewing them if they are to be kept for longer periods of time. Annual renewal helps avoid losing contact with lenders who move, since the post office will forward mail for one year. Someone on the staff should be responsible for updating the loans every year; a tickler file, a loan list in an action folder or a computer task file helps bring loan deadlines to a museum worker's attention. The museum should update both its incoming and outgoing long-term loans consistently.

Another way of tackling the problem is to change all loans to expire in a single month. Choose the month that is quietest, and when new loans are received or existing loans come for renewal, make them for a duration that expires in the chosen month. If loan renewal month is July and a new loan is negotiated in May, the initial loan agreement should show a term of 14 months. This uniformity should make renewals easier in the long run.

No one system is used by all museums, but a combination of reliable first-time record keeping, as noted above, and consistent updating will usually avoid old loans.

Notes

1. "Everything that looks like it might be part of the collection" could include material brought to the museum for a workshop or an appraisal day. In these cases, especially one-day events, it is possible to simplify systems so that what comes in goes out with its owner. If the museum accepts an object for identification or examination, it should be thoroughly processed so that it can be tracked within the museum and returned to its owner when the activity is complete.

2. Letters indicate inseparable parts of a whole unit, while numbers indicate discreet elements that can be exhibited individually.

4: Case Studies

NORTHWEST MUSEUM OF ARTS AND CULTURE: COMPLEXITY AND CARE IN THE INLAND NORTHWEST

Rebecca A. Buck

The Eastern Washington State Historical Society (EWSHS), which operates as the Northwest Museum of Art and Culture (MAC), in Spokane Wash. presents a complex pattern of collecting history, mergers, building acquisition and collection development. During its 90-year history it has subsumed the collections of one museum, merged with another, had three major building additions and has restored and maintains a historic house. It also engages in custodial relationships with Native American tribes and a local museum. It was early to recognize and begin to reconcile collections problems, and it continues to refine its collections and increase knowledge and awareness of Native American and Inland Northwest culture and art. I thank Larry Schoonover, director of exhibits and programs; Laura Thayer, curator of collections; and Rose Krause, curator of special collections, for their help and hospitality.

Spokan Falls, just west of Washington's border with Idaho, lay in a protected valley. With a strong river and falls offering both scenic beauty and power, the city became a lively frontier town after its founding in 1872. It provided services for miners and farmers, foresters and financiers. On August 4, 1889, a fire devastated the town and burnt down 32 square blocks of the city center. The apocryphal story goes that the telegraphs whirled through the night, telling the story so many times that "Spokan Falls became Spokane," thus making it forever difficult for non-natives to properly pronounce the city's name.

Spokane was well placed to become an important regional center. It was close to Idaho's wealthy Coeur d'Alene mines, there was tremendous potential for agriculture in the rolling hills of the Palouse to the south and the Rockies to the east provided timber for building and paper-making. So Spokane became the queen city of the old Inland Empire, now the Inland Northwest, that is composed of inland Washington and Oregon and northern Idaho. The earliest native residents of this vast area, the Spokane, were part of the Plateau Region, with Coeur d'Alene, Nez Perce, Colville, Yakima and others. They remain a strong force in the region.

Northwest Museum of Arts and Culture—The MAC. Courtesy of the Eastern Washington State Historical Society.

The western bluffs of the city, overlooking the Spokane River, became known as Browne's Addition after J. J. Browne, a lawyer from Portland, Oregon, who bought a quarter interest in the Spokane townsite from James Glover and chose that spot for his own home. In the 1890s the wealth increased as railroad, mines, retail stores and real estate grew in value. Browne's Addition became a neighborhood of stately homes, and the "Age of Elegance" was underway. In 1898 Amasa Campbell, a businessman with strong interests in the mines, built an English Tudor Revival home with rooms reminiscent of different countries. The Campbell House was home to Amasa and Grace Campbell and their daughter Helen.

Kirtland C. Cutter, the architect who rebuilt Spokane after the 1889 fire, designed the Campbell house as well as several other homes in the neighborhood. The reception room is French rococo, gilded and red, with white woodwork; Grace, Amasa's wife, met her visitors there. The library has dark oak and a Gothic style; the family used it for informal gatherings. The dining room was decorated with blue and white tile and was formally set with a table and 12 chairs. There was a

gaming room in the basement for Amasa and his friends to hold card games and play billiards. The house had a central hot water system and electric as well as gas fixtures. Servants, carriages and a pony cart and European travel were part and parcel of the Campbells' lives during the early years of the twentieth century.

In 1912 Amasa Campbell died, and his wife continued to live in the house with Helen. On June 27, 1917, Helen married William Powell in the library. In 1924 Grace Campbell died after a long decline, and Helen gave the home to the Eastern Washington State Historical Society.

The residents of Spokane were interested in history and art from the town's founding. On April 20, 1916, several citizens, after a meeting of the Inland Empire Teachers Association, founded the Spokane Historical Society. It was officially incorporated on June 5, 1916.

Historical societies often develop museums, and the Spokane Historical Society began almost immediately to show a few curios in a case in a room in the Spokane city hall. The collections, owned by W. W. Manning, were on loan, but were later a major purchase for the society's muse-

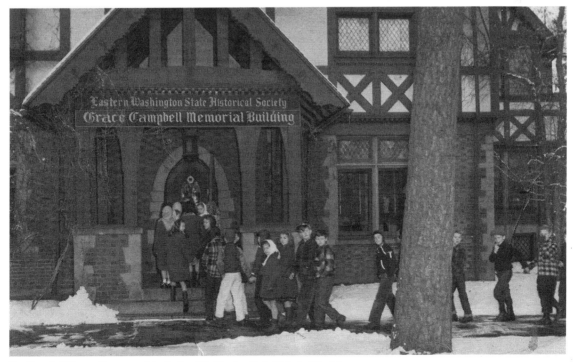

The Campbell House. Courtesy of the Eastern Washington State Historical Society.

um. Following the accessioning system of libraries of the age, the Manning accession was listed as accession number 1. From 1916 to the present, accessioning has been by sequential number, with objects given individual numbers by adding a second part, i.e. 1.1, 1.2, etc.

Accession Numbers for Loans

Conundrum!

Are accession numbers given to loans?

Laurence Vail Coleman, whose *Manual for Small Museums* was published in 1927, notes that "an accession, by definition, is a batch of material received at one time from one source. It represents a single transaction and may include one object or many. The material need not be an acquisition; it may be received on approval or loan; it may be a traveling exhibit." This process was the working norm in some museums in the early part of the 20th century, and the Manning accession, listed as number 1, is listed as a loan in the accession register. It was purchased many years later and retained the same number. The practice of giving accession numbers to loans or exhibits was discontinued in most American museums later in the century and was never used in some. Temporary Custody Receipt or Temporary Receipt numbers are generally used for anything not owned by a museum.

The society's museum made several moves, from Norfolk Hall in 1917 to a room at the Crescent Department Store, the only building in the downtown area to survive the 1889 fire. A Crescent advertisement noted: "Begun a few years ago with a handful of relics of pioneer days, the society's collection has grown in size and importance until it includes not only items from the Northwest, but has valuable specimens from every part of the world and from every prehistoric age, as well as from ancient, medieval and modern times."[1] The patterns of collecting, so far from the core of

museums in the northeastern part of the country, nevertheless echoed those museums. Human nature, regardless of place and, to some extent, time, showed the same desire to see natural curios and historic relics. In addition, in the far west, even though western history was short, there were nearby collections of Native American artifacts.

In 1918 the society amended the Articles of Incorporation to change the name of the Society to the Eastern Washington State Historical Society (EWSHS); it was the first in a long series of name changes. The museum would soon ask for state aid but would not become state-funded for decades.

The tight quarters at the Crescent gave way to a place at the Wharton Block, and by 1921 it was reported that there were 28,960 objects in the collection. The collections were primarily historical objects, natural history specimens, and Native American artifacts, notwithstanding a generous group of curios and relics.

Mrs. Burgess Lee Gordon became president of the society around 1924, and she was also heavily involved in the Spokane Art Association. She wanted to unite art and history in the Spokane museum, and was able in 1925 to announce an amalgamation of the two disciplines when Helen Campbell Powell donated the Campbell House for art exhibits, with the society retaining offices and showing history exhibits on the second floor.

It did indeed become a community museum. The walls on the second floor were eventually torn out to produce a large room dedicated to a worldwide mineral collection, and the carriage house gave way eventually to exhibitions of taxidermied animals and birds including Little Miracle, a young elephant born in Montana, which lived only a few months. The society had gone far beyond history and become a true general museum for the city.

In 1926 EWSHS was officially recognized by the State of Washington and made a "trustee of the people" to collect materials relevant to the state. Funding from the state, however, did not arrive until 1937 when the state appropriated $10,000 for operations and maintenance of the museum.

Collecting and expansion continued during the next two decades. Mr. and Mrs. W. W. Powell (Helen Campbell Powell) donated land adjacent to Campbell House in memory of their son, who died in World War II. Joel E. Ferris, head of the building committee, was instrumental in working with the Cowles family in their donation of money for a building in memory of Major Cheney Cowles. The new building, the Cheney Cowles Memorial Museum (CCMM), opened in 1960 and included the Joel E. Ferris Research Library and Archives. Campbell House began its long return to the former "Age of Elegance," as small steps were taken. A formal restoration from 1984–2001 changed the structures and furnishings as well as the landscape and brought back the integrity of the house; additions of furniture and other decorative arts occur as pieces are found. An addition to the CCMM was begun in 1984 as well, and the Eastern Washington Museum Foundation was created to provide private support for a museum now supported primarily by state funding.

Finding a need for more space, the society spent several years exploring expansion. A commitment to AAM's Excellence and Equity program was made in 1993 when the museum conducted a community-driven pre-design study. In 1999, EWSHS received an $18.7 million capital appropriation from the state of Washington to build "A Museum for the New Millennium." The Cheney Cowles Memorial Museum was remodeled to become the Cheney Cowles Center, the site used for storage, library and archives, and administrative offices. A new museum, with café, museum store, an outdoor amphitheater and five exhibition galleries was built. A new name came with the new building—Northwest Museum of Arts and Culture, known as "the MAC." The new facility opened in 2001.

The history of the museum is complex, and that of its collection is even more difficult to follow. The collection has been constantly reshaped throughout the history of the institution, and the museum has often been in the forefront of professional movements to clarify collection title as well as to proceed with thoughtful deaccession. It was one of the early museums to seek accreditation from the American Association of Museums in 1972, and it has also been among the first to embrace the idea of clear collecting guidelines.

Three intertwined forces worked to shape the museum and its collections over the years: the evolving mission of the museum, progressive and professional staffing that gave the museum the ability to stay in tune with national developments in the museum community and the greater American culture and the financial stability of an institution strongly supported by the community and by the state of Washington. The museum's environment allowed for inclusion of major collections from one museum that was closing, virtual merger with another and ongoing custodial relationships with a third museum, as well as several Native American tribes; it also prompted the museum continually to refine its collections by loan conversion, deaccession and, most importantly, thoughtful collecting.

Mission and Staff

As the society aged, its mission statement changed several times. Each time, a major shift in the mode of collecting and dealing with the collection occurred as well. Collections went from loosely controlled general collections to very well defined regional collections and back to more loosely defined collections. Each time, the mission of the society mirrored trends occurring in the national museum community, illustrating the progression of ways museums have viewed themselves in the United States.

The object of the Eastern Washington State Historical Society, 1918, reads:

> *To gather and preserve all manner of objects, illustrative of the various phases of natural and human history, and for that purpose to establish and maintain at the City of Spokane, a free public museum for the exhibition and display of such objects, for the benefit and education of the citizens of the State of Washington, and especially of school children, students and scientists.*

Enabling legislation, January 20, 1926:

The Eastern Washington State Historical Society is designated a trustee of the state of Washington to maintain and preserve, for the use and benefit of the people of the state, those articles and properties which illustrate the history of the state (RCW 27.34).

Mission statement, late 1970s:

The mission of the Eastern Washington State Historical Society is to collect, preserve, and interpret the history of eastern Washington and the Inland Empire; and to collect, preserve, and interpret visual arts of regional, national, and international importance.

Mission Statement, June 28, 1994:

The Mission of the Eastern Washington State Historical Society is to actively engage the people of the Inland Northwest in life-long learning about regional history; visual arts; and American Indian and other cultures, especially those specific to the region. The Society fulfills its mission by collecting, preserving, and interpreting relevant material and by involving and stimulating people through integrated exhibits and programs.

Mission statement, 2004:

The mission of the Eastern Washington State Historical Society (MAC) is to actively engage all people in the appreciation of arts and culture through collections stewardship, exhibits, and programs that educate and entertain.

The Board of Trustees of the Eastern Washington State Historical Society has been strong and involved over its many decades. From the will to bring history and art together, shown by Mrs. Burgess Lee Gordon in the 1920s, to the successful campaign to build a new facility in the first decade of the twenty-first century, the society and its programs have constantly been reshaped. The society has always, as well, been in stride with emerging professional culture in the museum world.

As noted above, it was reported that there were 28,960 objects in the collections by 1921. There is also a record of rooms in exhibitions being inventoried in the 1930s. The first complete and reconciled inventory, however, was done in 1978, and listed 46,549 objects. With the later inclusion of many objects from the Ft. Wright Museum (1,459 objects) and the collections of the Museum of Native American Culture, which had approximately 38,000 objects, and the addition of new acquisitions from all other sources, it would be logical that the collections of the museum must be well over 100,000 in number. Indeed, the introduction to a deaccession booklet published in 1991 notes that more than 100,000 objects had been taken into the museum over the years. In 2005, though, the staff reported that there are perhaps 36,000 objects in the current collection. It takes an active and selective stance to continually examine and re-examine and to cull a large collection so that the remaining core materials are those of most use to the museum and its community; this is precisely what the MAC has done.

How Do You Count Museum Objects?

Conundrum!

Any count of museum objects must be taken only as an approximation. Beyond the simpler problems, such as a pair of shoes being 1 or 2 and a standard deck of cards being 1 or 52 objects, are an endless series of wonderful counting problems for museum staff. Did 1 piece of mica split into 10 pieces? When the archaeological series of beads are strung as they were originally, do they go from 100 objects back to 1 object? Should each watercolor in an artist's sketchbook be counted separately, or should the sketchbook count as 1 object? Even Noah Webster could get totally confused trying to deal with these numbers on a daily basis. Databases don't help either because decisions to break out parts of objects must be made on whether or not they may develop a slightly different history (location, conservation, exhibition) than their fellows. Even though talking about "whole" objects does not help—each watercolor in that sketchbook must be catalogued and photographed—it is probably best to estimate collection numbers with whole objects as opposed to anything that is in parts. The result will not be exact, or even particularly true, but the audience will have a general idea of the extent of the collection.

The 1978 inventory was completed long before computers were available. Inventories can be planned in many ways, and this one was planned from the beginning to be as simple and complete as possible. Its goal was not just to count and list objects, but to reconcile them definitively with the records on file. The inventory was characterized as necessary because "no one had faced the problems of the early records or had tried to inventory the collections systematically."[2]

To that end, photocopies of the listing of objects in more than 2,000 accession files were made, or, if listings were not simple, a typed list was made from the file. Those copies were put into a series of six or seven binders that were carted from room to room as the inventory progressed. Sixteen persons, fifteen of them volunteers, worked eight months to complete the inventory. They made direct comparisons of the objects on exhibit, on loan, and in storage to the objects listed in the notebook set, noting each as located (with location) or on loan (with the borrower noted). Objects with no numbers, or problem numbers that could not be found in the notebooks, were physically separated from inventoried objects.

The inventory led to four major projects:

a. Production of location card files that could be kept up-to-date with all future object moves.

b. Reworking of major files so that accession lists were comprehensive and minor problems were solved.

c. Beginning of serious loan conversion.

d. Reconciliation of undocumented objects.

The inventory proved useful in 1981 when the state of Washington confirmed that the society could exclude historical, artistic and museum artifacts from the property management system that the state implemented that year. The state asked that all formal procedures and policies relating to the museum's catalogue be sent for its file. The society sent those and noted that the first inventory was completed and that the process for future inventory would include general inventories at ten-year intervals and spot inventories in four to six locations per year.

Locations became more easily managed when the society implemented its first database for collections management in the 1990s. The general inventory, however, provided the basis for resolving many collections problems.

Loans and Old Loans

Early exhibits, such as the one from the Manning collection in 1917, held many loans, which were long an accepted form of expanding the base collections of museums. There was a period of time, from perhaps the early 1970s through the early 1990s, when the whole issue of loans was reviewed by the museum community and prevailing opinion turned against long-term loans. Issues of risk, space, staff time and limitations on use all had negative effects on maintaining loans for indefinite periods.

At some point, probably in the early 1940s, the Eastern Washington State Historical Society's "Public Museum" made its first effort at lessening the risk that ensues from holding loaned material. A letter to Delos Fowler, who had loaned material to the museum, notified him that loans left for more than 20 years would become the property of the museum. During World War II the society was having trouble getting adequate insurance, and Miss Arcola Glasgow wrote a general letter to lenders noting the new policy that the society could no longer insure loans:

It will be impossible for the Eastern Washington State Historical Society to carry insurance on loan exhibits in the future. Therefore, it is necessary for the owners of such exhibits to carry their own insurance, if such protection is desired.

The Trustees have recently passed a resolution that any loaned exhibitions remaining in the possession of the Public Museum for twenty years, automatically becomes the property of the Society.

You are hereby being notified of these changes.

There is no indication of any response to this letter. It is reminiscent of the wording on many current loan and temporary deposit forms. Museum professional staff seem always very careful to do whatever possible to protect the museum, and yet the result of the many steps taken is unseen. Unlike many museums, EWSHS actually acted upon its notice to lenders. In the unfortunate case of a theft, the following notice went out to a lender:

March 31, 1943

Mr. James E. Offutt
420 East 8th Avenue
Spokane, Washington

Dear Mr. Offutt:

We are very sorry to have to report to you that the brass pistol you loaned to the Museum has been stolen. We have tried our best to guard against such theft, but it just seems the small arms case is too much for some one. We have finally decided to store this material.

Your brass percussion lock pistol was loaned to us in 1922. You stated at that time that it had been taken off a drowned man found in the Ohio River.

While it is a ruling of the Museum that after loaned material has been left with us for twenty years it automatically becomes the property of the Historical Society, we thought it best to notify you of the loss.

Very sincerely,
Eastern Washington State Historical Society
Assistant Secretary

There are very few cases that involve individuals fighting in court for return of a loan or claiming something in a museum collection is theirs. There is no indication that the letter above was challenged, nor are there any challenges to the use of the old loan legislation in Washington. There are, however, instances where lenders or their heirs do seek the return of objects without resorting to legal action. One such case occurred in the late 1970s in Spokane when a lender's granddaughter appeared at the museum and requested that an organ loaned in 1917 be returned. Her proof of ownership was legitimate, the organ was found and the loan was returned.

The Washington state law covering old loans, passed in 1975 and applying only to the Burke Museum of the University of Washington, simply noted that unclaimed loans became property of the museum 90 days after actual notification of the lender. There was no indication of what to do should the lender not be found and nothing in the law that covered undocumented property. Other museums in the state, including the EWSHS, developed policies based on the legislation and tried to further amendments to include all historical societies and museums. The legislation was amended in 1988 and has been used to the society's advantage since that time.

There was a serious attempt at loan updates and conversions in 1970, and a second attempt followed the complete inventory of 1978. At that time it was determined that there were 266 "active" incoming loan transactions in the museum. A notebook was assembled that contained a cover page for each loan, on which was listed the dates and terms of the loans, the last known address of the lender and a list of objects. All actions were recorded in the notebook. The goal, because there was no loan conversion law that covered the museum at that time, was to return the loaned objects or convert them to gifts by negotiating with the original lender or the lender's heirs. Staff also suggested that adverse possession be used to try to claim loans as society material.

The process for converting loans, written by the registrar in 1978, follows:

Methods of Conversion or Return
The following steps may be taken in the converting of loan to gift material, or in having loan material withdrawn from the Museum:

a. *Review all loans in order to judge their current status.*

b. *Locate objects that are on loan, note location and condition.*

c. *If objects are found, make reasonable effort to determine and locate the legal owner.*

   If objects are missing (lost, stolen, or irreparably damaged) consult legal counsel for steps to be taken.

d. *Determine and locate legal owners.*

   If owner is still living, determine last address which it is possible to find.

   If owner is deceased, simple probate search is possible.

e. *Convert the loan to a gift or return it to the owner.*

Letters to legal owners will explain, in as positive way as possible, reasons for the conversion or withdrawal. If the objects involved are of importance to the museum, statements about benefit to the museum and possible tax deductions will be included. If the objects are a burden to the museum, a simple request for withdrawal will be made. Importance of objects can be determined by the director, respective curators, and librarian. If the Board wishes, the Accessions Committee may be involved in such decisions.

In general, the loan return process began by trying to contact each lender. If a registered letter, the actual notice, was delivered to the lender and communications were opened, negotiations about the loan could begin. If the letter was returned, the next step was to search all available sources for the lender. Phone books were consulted first, and people with the same or very similar names or addresses were contacted. Most lenders were local to the Spokane area, so if there was no entry in the phone directories, the city directories and the archives of the two local newspapers, the *Chronicle* and the *Spokesman-Review*, were searched. If obituaries were found, the trail led to the Spokane County Court House, where wills were read and heirs determined. In some cases death certificates were ordered to try to learn more of relatives. The process, after finding heirs, repeated from the beginning.

In 1991 the society converted title on several loans using that 1988 amended law. In 2005 there were 144 loans still on the books at the museum. The current collections policy states that "No indefinite or long-terms loans shall be routinely accepted. The board of trustees with the recommendation of the CEO may authorize exceptions." Although there has been a swing back toward the use of long-term loans by museums to "complete" permanent exhibitions, most policies of museums contain something similar to this. In addition, most museums now require that any long-term loan be renewed annually. Current EWSHS policy does allow the society to enter into custodial relationships with tribal groups, museums or institutions with similar missions.

Undocumented Objects and Found in Collection

After the 1978 inventory was completed, all undocumented objects were placed in one storage location. There were more than 2,000 such objects, and more than 2,000 objects that were not located during the inventory. A separate listing of these lost in inventory objects was made for fast reference, culled from the notebooks used for the inventory.

Unfortunately, as in many museums started at the beginning of the twentieth century, the entries in accession ledgers and on catalogue cards are far from definitive. For example:

4.9	Vase
5.28	Orange rind tray
19.1	Gun
39.3.40	BPOE 148, card with lavender ribbon
41.24	Vegetable dish

Needless to say, the only object marked as found when reconciliation began was 39.3.40, because the description is extensive enough to match. The card and its documentation were reunited.

The process for reconciling these objects was very physical. Objects of a type were sorted out and placed on tables—all dolls, for instance, or all war paraphernalia. They were then reviewed and compared to the lost in inventory list. There are often, in this type of process, some tempting matches that might be made. A brown tray is found. Is it the orange rind tray? Was that tray made of orange rinds or made to hold them? Curiosity or utilitarian artifact? An attempt was made to err always on the conservative side and not match objects unless there were clear indicators.

When as much reconciliation was done as possible, the remaining objects, now clearly found-in-collection objects, were accessioned. Before the inventory and reconciliation, everything had been given an N (no number) number for tracking purposes. After the reconciliation process, the remaining objects were given the next consecutive catalogue numbers by material type and considered to be the same as other accessioned objects.

The drawback of the manual system was the inability to search all types of information to find the match between object and documentation. In 1994 the curator of collections was finishing the NAGPRA (Native American Graves Protection and Repatriation Act) inventory when she came across a box of five Native American objects with a note from 1978 saying that they could not be reconciled with existing documentation. They provide a good lesson in why it is important to keep all records made by an institution, never to retire numbers or deaccession objects that are lost in inventory and to keep all of that information in a database.

The objects included a bone awl, a porcupine quill, a Plateau horsehair bridle, a Navajo bridle of leather and iron and a wampum necklace. With a database now in place, it took a staff member only 30 minutes to match those pieces with records from the late 1910s on. Some of those pieces had been without documentation for perhaps 75 years.

THE LURE OF THE RELIC

The Northwest Museum of Arts and Culture (the MAC) has had its share of relics over the decades, from a piece of "Old Ironsides" to an Egyptian mummy's foot to the "hand of the man who shed his skin." These objects, fitted to the curiosity cabinets of an age long gone (and to the early mission of the museum), have either been deaccessioned or remain unused. There are some relics, however, like the two shown here, that tell a larger story and become interesting parts of a museum collection. As noted in a collection statement from the society, they "put the Inland Empire in context."

E. BIEBER HAMBURG
K. HOF- PHOTOGRAPHIN NEUER JUNGFERNSTIEG, 20.

Trapeze artist Leona Dare. Courtesy of John Culme.

When Spokane was just beginning, Leona Dare was already famous. Known as "The Comet of 1873" she rose above the cities of Europe, hanging only by her teeth from hot air balloons. Dare, born Susan Adeline Stuart in 1855, was a child of the Civil War who ran away to join the circus. She met Thomas Hall, a.k.a. Thomas Dare, marrying him in 1871, and became an aerialist. She moved on to more daring feats and a second husband, and became known for her fearlessness and for several accidents. Once she was said to have been frightened by a balloon that was running amok, causing her to let go and fall, breaking her leg. A second accident was reported as follows:

> Lately, at the Princess's Theatre, Valencia, Spain, Leona Dare, the American acrobat, was suspended from the roof of the theatre by her feet, and held in her teeth the ropes of a trapeze-bar on which a male acrobat, known as M. George, was performing. During the act Miss Dare was seized with a nervous fit and dropped the trapeze. M. George and the apparatus dropped whirling to the floor. The audience were horror-stricken. Every one rushed for the doors, and a panic ensued, in which many people were crushed and otherwise injured. Miss Dare clung to the roof, screaming hysterically. She was rescued with difficulty after the excitement had somewhat subsided, and is now confined to her bed from exhaustion following the shock. M. George has since, by cable, been reported dead, and Miss Dare in a precarious condition.
> —The *Entr'acte*, London, Saturday, 13 December 1884, p.13b

When her career ended, Leona Dare moved to Spokane, where members of her family lived. She remained there, well away from the bright lights and bustle, until her death in 1922. Buried in Riverside Cemetery in Spokane, where she is called Madame Leona Dare, she has become a footnote to the history of the Northwest. In 1981, Dare's nieces, Jeanne Keck and Barbara

Oehler of Spokane, gave the MAC a collection of costumes and artifacts that had belonged to their aunt. Exhibitions of the material, presented when it arrived and again in 2005, celebrate not only Dare but also the history of entertainment in the frontier town. The artifacts include costumes and jewelry, slippers, autographs and perhaps the most exciting piece—the mouthpiece from which she hung.

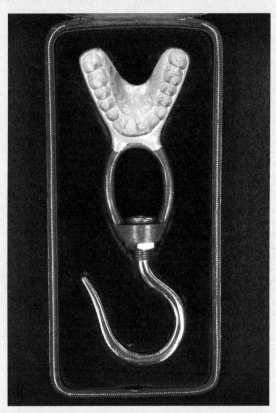

Leona Dare's Mouthpiece. Courtesy of the Eastern Washington State Historical Society.

2790.7a,b   Aeronaut Mouthpiece in case. Case 8 ¾ x 4 1/8 x 1 ¾ in. Mouthpiece 7 3/8 x 2 ½ x 1 3/8 in. Steel and ceramic mouthpiece. Steel hook attached to an impression of the inside of Leona Dare's mouth and teeth. Impression painted pink. Case is black leather with deep red satin and velvet lining. Alexandres, DANTON SCCT, 21 Rue Auber, 21 Pa

Deaccessions

After the society decided to become more regional in its mission in the late 1970s, it deaccessioned a vast quantity of material from the Pacific rim, or Oceania. Most of that material was sent to the University of Washington's Burke Museum in Seattle, Washington. In addition, African material was deaccessioned and the Accessions Committee began turning down gifts that did not have the requisite regional credentials.

One large collection of African musical instruments was deaccessioned in the late 1970s. After careful review, the board determined that the material could be given back to the original donors, African missionaries, who had not taken a tax deduction at the time of the gift. Oddly enough, one of the staff members who worked on the deaccession moved several years later to a university museum that was called one day by those same donors. They offered the exact collection to the university museum, which accepted it. The former EWSHS registrar used the deaccession and inventory notes on file to pack and ship the material to its new museum home.

In an extremely innovative move, EWSHS decided in 1991 to undertake a major local and public deaccessioning process in order to cull non-relevant objects from the collection, and to raise money for acquisitions and direct collection care. Most museums are hesitant to go public with deaccessioning, fearing bad publicity, but the society's Cheney Cowles Museum laid careful foundations for the auction and made it very public. This arose in part from necessity, since Spokane is 350 miles from Seattle, 1,500 from Minneapolis and is the largest city between the two. There was no simple way for deaccessioned objects to disappear in a small auctions several cities over; the process had to be local and straightforward in order to be practical.

The stage was set with careful cataloguing and review of objects in the collections. Several title conversions were done. A revision of Washington state's 1975 legislation became inclusive and in 1988 became "an act relating to unclaimed property in museums and historical societies." That act pertains to both undocumented unclaimed property and old loans. It requires actual notice if an owner of the property is known and can be located or constructive notice if those conditions cannot be met. That notice, publication for two consecutive weeks in newspapers in the county in which the museum sits and the county in which the owner was last known to reside, is followed by a very short, 90-day waiting period before the museum may claim the property as its own.

The auction took place at the local Masonic Temple over two days and raised $100,000. The accompanying catalogue explained that "deaccessioning is the formal process of removing items from a museum's permanent collection." It explained the various reviews and approvals each object was subjected to before it was included in the deaccession auction.

The brochure also included an overview of collecting in the first 75 years of the society's history, noting that approximately one hundred thousand objects had been accepted during that time. It published and discussed the society's mission statement and the need to maintain collections related to that mission, not the collections that "only had curiosity appeal; [or] others [that] were not of exhibitable quality or duplicated items already in the collection."[3] The booklet also outlined the collecting guidelines and encouraged the public to donate materials that aligned with the mission of the society and would be useful for exhibition and study.

This deaccessioning process was multifaceted: old title problems were cleared, objects that were taking space and money not fitting the mission of the institution were deaccessioned and sold, money was raised and best of all, the public was educated.

Mergers and Inclusions

The Eastern Washington State Historical Society was, from its beginnings in 1916, the largest and best supported museum in the Inland Northwest. In the 1960s two other museums were organized in

Spokane and opened their doors: the Fort George Wright Historical Museum and the Museum of Native American Cultures (MONAC).

Fort George Wright, in the area of Spokane originally known as Twickenham Park, was built between 1897 and 1906 and was used for military purposes until 1957. When it was decommissioned, the government gave educational institutions priority for purchase of the property. Holy Names College, a liberal arts college for women, purchased and used 76 acres. That college, later renamed Fort Wright College, operated until 1982.

Fort Wright College organized a historical museum in 1964, and it, too, operated until the college closed in 1982. Its mission was "to collect, preserve, and display material relating to the physical occupancy of the Fort." When it closed, the Eastern Washington State Historical Society received most of the manuscript and photograph collections that had been held by the college museum. The society was also given the opportunity of taking in the whole material collection.

The tradition of careful and selective collecting that had been established at EWSHS

continued through this acquisition opportunity. Museum staff reviewed the collection, brought in material on loan for further evaluation, and between June 3 and October 9, 1982, received chosen material as a gift. The Fort Wright collection was culled to 1,372 artifacts, which were processed at the museum as a single accession, as any other gift transaction would be, and received accession number 2962.

MONAC, loosely associated with Gonzaga University on the east side of Spokane, involved a much more complicated transaction. Rather than being a fairly straightforward, large gift, MONAC, upon its closure in 1991, dissolved and merged its collections and remaining assets into the Eastern Washington State Historical Society.

Museum of Native American Cultures

The Museum of Native American Cultures (MONAC) was founded in 1965 and run by the Pacific Northwest Indian Center. MONAC's mission was to collect and display objects of

The Museum of Native American Cultures. Courtesy of the Eastern Washington State Historical Society.

Native American culture as well as historical documents relating to the American West and the fur trade; it collected, in its short history, more than 38,000 objects.

When it became apparent that MONAC could not maintain financial independence, it entered into a contract with EWSHS. The reasons for MONAC's closure were many. The collections of the two museums, in some part, duplicated each other with large and important collections of Native American material. MONAC was concerned about its facility and expressed fear that the collections would deteriorate without proper maintenance and upgrading of the building. EWSHS, on the other hand, had just upgraded to state-of-the-art systems.

The MONAC dissolution document noted the history of the organization and outlined its preferences for future treatment of its collections: the society should add board members who were familiar with MONAC; the society was encouraged to develop and maintain close relationships with Native Americans in the Inland Northwest; all revenues that might be realized from disposition of non-relevant materials should be restricted to acquisition of Native American objects or care and conservation of the Native American collections; collections from MONAC should be credited to MONAC (Gift of Joe Smith, MONAC, Northwest Museum of Arts and Culture). The society took over the gift shop, furniture and all MONAC funds that were extant. The collections and their documentation were transferred.

Again, as it had been with Fort Wright, care was taken to make certain that the collections accepted were selected only after serious review. The contract stipulated:

> It is understood that the Society has the right to determine which objects and collections from MONAC are suitable for accessioning into the Society's permanent collections. Objects of poor quality, over duplication, or irrelevant to the revised mission of the Society may be disposed of in the best interests of the Society and its American Indian collections.

The process that had been used in selecting objects, evaluating existing collections for duplication and researching historical importance, as well as assessing quality, was used again when the MONAC objects were transferred. The process has taken many years, and there are still remaining object decisions to be made. In the midst of the transfer, to complicate and prolong it, a vast project to change the campus and build a new building for exhibition galleries took place. In 2005 the society showed that 7,772 MONAC objects had entered the collections.

Custodial Relationships

To acknowledge and honor the cultures that made the Plateau and other American Indian material in the collection, the society keeps a separate room for sacred material that must be treated according to the customs of the individual tribes. An antechamber to that room can be used for ceremonies involving the objects within.

Several custodial agreements are maintained with regional Native Americans: Spokane, Coeur d'Alene and Kalispel. The collection policy indicates that "the Society may enter into custodial agreements with tribal groups, museums, or institutions with missions similar to the Society in order to protect and preserve materials and objects that are relevant to the mission of the Society." Tribal groups do fund some of the care and storage of their objects. Some groups wish to develop their own museums and eventually have their cultural artifacts returned; others will probably leave the material with the EWSHS for a very long time.

One museum, the former Fairchild Heritage Museum, now the Aerospace and Armed Forces Museum, also has a collection now in the custody of the society. That museum was developed to collect artifacts from the history of the Fairchild Air Force Base located near Spokane. In addition, the society, as a repository for the state of Washington, also holds some archaeological materials and artifacts from historic sites. Spokane House material, for instance, was deposited by the State Parks Board.

Collecting Guidelines

Two EWSHS staff members attended the Collecting Guidelines symposium held by the American Association of Museums in 2004, and work is underway to develop an even more comprehensive collecting plan. A committee comprised of educators, staff and community members will review the direction and future needs for collection development so that an intellectual framework can be established.

As noted above, EWSHS has already shown careful stewardship in its collecting and deaccessioning practices. When its mission changed in the late 1970s it deaccessioned non-regional artifacts. In 1991, it began another long process of deaccessioning, and in the brochure for the 1991 auction it placed a strong collecting statement that can now serve as a core collecting guideline.

What Do the Society and Its Museum Collect?

The Collection Policy emphasizes that the history, research library and Campbell house programs shall seek out items that:

- Contribute to the documentation and interpretation of the history and prehistory of the Inland Empire and its residents

- Put the Inland Empire in context with the state, region or nation

- Accurately furnish Campbell House, circa 1912

A separate statement defined the type of Inland Empire and Northwest art that was sought for the collection. The announcement ended with a call for donations of material relevant to the society.

The MAC is a complex museum. The Campbell House as museum has transformed into a recreation of the original nineteenth-century mansion, restored to 1912, the year that Amasa Campbell died. The Campbell Carriage House, once full of taxidermied birds and mammals, has been cleared for use as an orientation center for the house. The Cheney Cowles Memorial Museum opened in 1960 to provide exhibit and storage space for the collections and for the Joel E. Ferris Library, which is now the Cheney Cowles Center; a walkway that connected it to the Campbell House and obscured architectural detail is gone. Staff, collections storage, the library and the Art at Work program are based in the Center. MONAC and Fort Wright collections have blended into the early collections of the museum. The MAC's museum building is to the east, built down the cliff with columns mimicking the tall pines in the area. It houses shops, a café and expanded exhibition space. It is all legally still the Eastern Washington State Historical Society.

The collections have changed over the years as well. The curios and relics are mostly gone, as are the natural history collections. Oceania material and many of the natural history specimens are on loan to the Burke Museum at the University of Washington. Objects coming into the collection are carefully selected, and those already there are given careful housing in a properly conditioned environment. Collecting guidelines are being refined along AAM standards. The exhibits reflect the mission, and thus the collections. The museum has remained progressive; it provides the community with thoughtful exhibits and the region with a safe haven for its history and its artifacts.

ACCESSIONING THE N. C. WYETH HOUSE AND STUDIO

Jean Allman Gilmore

Contrary to the impression its name gives, the Brandywine River Museum in Chadds Ford, Pa., does not collect rivers, streams, creeks, brooks or runs. It is an art museum that focuses on art produced in the Brandywine Valley, American illustration, still lifes and landscapes. Its permanent collection consists, with few exceptions, of two-dimensional works on paper, canvas, panel in pencil, pen and ink, print media, watercolor, oil and egg tempera. The collection benefits from records of remarkable consistency and uniformity because in the span of time since the institution opened in 1971, it has had only two individuals charged with accessioning and collection record keeping.

To give context to works of art in its collection, the Brandywine River Museum accumulated a small number of objects of artist's memorabilia but did not face great challenges in cataloguing, housing or accounting for them; they were simply tracked as part of the library collection. In 1994, however, this situation changed with the bequest of artist N. C. Wyeth's house and studio from his daughter Carolyn. Suddenly, the museum's collection expanded six-fold to include a wealth of historic artifacts, including props, costumes and artist's materials; books, motion picture films and photographs; furniture, household goods and thousands of large and small items from the family's daily life. As registrar, I was accustomed to accessioning one or a few—only on the

rare occasion a few hundred—objects at a time, assigning and affixing an accession number to each one, completing an accession sheet, setting up an object file with ownership documents and reporting accessions quarterly to the board of trustees for acceptance into the permanent collection. I now faced the task of accessioning nearly ten thousand diverse, historic artifacts, a situation akin to discovering an eight-foot polar bear in the parlor. Taming the huge beast demanded a fresh strategy. I started with the Wyeth studio.

When we first entered N. C. Wyeth's studio in 1995, it seemed untouched since the artist himself had walked out of it for the last time in October 1945. Of course, we knew this was not the case. For one thing, an estate appraiser had been through, pulling objects out of cupboards and drawers and moving things around. And we knew that the studio had been used off and on

N. C. Wyeth's studio. Courtesy of the Brandywine River Museum.

over the years by other members of this artistic family; Carolyn Wyeth taught art classes there for many years, for example. We knew also that certain key items from the studio had been moved to Harrisburg in the 1970s to recreate N. C. Wyeth's studio for an exhibition at the Pennsylvania State Museum. The Miss Havisham's dining-room aspect of the studio resulted from the fact that it had not been modified, renovated or even cleaned very often over the years. It had received basic maintenance to keep the roof sound and the furnace functioning, but shelves of books and chests and stacks of materials were still roughly where they had been in N. C. Wyeth's time.

Dirt and pest damage were key enemies to combat. Books, for example, had a thick layer of dust on the top edge, making us reluctant to open them to place numbers inside and collect basic catalogue information lest we scatter the dirt among the pages. A prop and frame storage room attached to the rear of the studio had suffered water damage, collapsing the floor under a loaded bookcase. Repairing that breach and closing other entryways for varmints was the first item on the agenda of our facilities maintenance staff, who sought the services of a restoration carpenter to make repairs in keeping with the style and appearance of the historic structure.

To tackle the enormous task of accessioning studio contents, we acquired a computer and a collections management database and hired Ruth Power. We told her the job would be data entry, but it turned out to involve much more, including such tasks as vacuuming mouse nests from inside trunks and cabinets. Her most startling encounter occurred as she pulled books off the shelf over the collapsed floor to make way for the carpenter and found two peacefully sleeping snakes. Amazingly, she returned the next day to continue assigning and affixing numbers to objects one by one, measuring them, photographing them and creating a record for each in the database.

We contracted with conservators to remove the grime of decades and pack each item for temporary storage. Technicians from the Conservation

Center for Art and Historic Artifacts performed initial cleaning and produced a preliminary conservation assessment of the books. Objects conservator Kory Berrett set up a field conservation lab in the anteroom, placing a portable utility sink outside for washing objects because there was no running water at the studio. Kory's wife, Pat Keller, a historian and freelance curator, assisted him in processing the objects and added valuable information to the database, identifying makers, materials, uses and dates wherever possible. Her expertise nicely supplemented our staff curators, who are exclusively art historians.

Eventually, everything was recorded, washed, assessed and packed away. Objects made of organic materials were placed in a freezer truck, rented for the occasion, to rid them of insect infestations. The empty studio was then washed down and repaired as needed. We made a decision, for the sake of preservation and historicity, not to put a fresh coat of paint on everything, but instead carefully cleaned walls and woodwork and applied paint only where it was needed, tinted to match the existing color.

Christine Podmaniczky, our associate curator who had for several years been assembling a catalogue raisonné of N. C. Wyeth's work, took over management of the studio. She arranged for further conservation and the repair of items that were to be displayed in the recreated studio and returned materials to their 1945 places, as shown in archival photographs, which someone with great foresight took soon after the artist's death. Storage space was created in the attic of the barn on the premises for those materials not included in the studio's final presentation.

The studio opened to the public in the summer of 1996, and Ruth Power moved her data entry operation to the N. C. Wyeth house. Because the house had been continuously occupied by Wyeth family members, objects there did not know the same level of benign neglect as those in the studio. We discarded post-1945 items, such as television sets, and proceeded with conservation on an individual basis rather than as a full-scale campaign. The house was added to the public tour in 1997.

Our approach to cataloguing this mass of material was simply to begin at one end and work to the other. Ruth created an individual data record for each item as well as "set" records where needed to connect objects that together composed a unit. She recorded basic object information, original location (even though the object might have been moved by family members or by the estate appraiser) and the box into which it was packed for temporary storage. As the studio was reassembled, locations were updated to reflect assigned exhibition or storage areas.

We created a collection separate from the permanent collection, assigning to these objects the prefix NCWS for N. C. Wyeth Studio, followed by 1995 (the year in which we expected to take ownership) and sequential numbers thereafter. Occasionally, when we came to a large group of items, such as glass lantern slides, we gave them the same number and added a fourth element for individual items; for example, NCWS.1995.1825.1–444. We did this to allow us to move ahead and return later to complete individual cataloguing. It also made it easier to bring together like items that had been scattered over the years.

Although we accessioned the bequest as a 1995 acquisition, ownership was not legally transferred until 1996. We elected to retain the number 1995 for already accessioned objects, rather than remove and repaint numbers on thousands of objects. Works of art that came with the bequest had not yet been accessioned and so were given 1996 numbers in the permanent collection sequence and reported to the board of trustees in the appropriate quarter. Our sophisticated database accommodates these irregularities.

Our original intent was to number items in the N. C. Wyeth House with the prefix NCWH; however, it soon became apparent that over the years objects had migrated from one building to the other. Since we had no functional need to make a distinction between house and studio, all objects received the same prefix.

Physical files have been created only for documents related to the bequest and for items that have received further conservation or research. Basic catalogue and accession files of this collection, however, exist only in (well backed up!) electronic form.

We continue to receive gifts to the studio collection from members of the Wyeth family: Mrs. N. C. Wyeth's formal dresses; N. C.'s smock, palette and firearm and edged weapon collection; and the teddy bear of one of the children, among other donations. These gifts are received by a variation of the standard gift agreement, which states that they are given to the studio collection. Unless there is a gift of unusual interest, these acquisitions are reported to the board of trustees informally, via the director's annual "status of collections" report. The entire house, studio and contents were presented, without being itemized, to the board as an acquisition in 1996. Any objects turning up later, as well as subsequent gifts, are deemed to have been included in the original board resolution to accept the collection.

The accessioning of the studio collection was an eye-opening, mind-expanding experience. The very acquisition of all these "things" made me more receptive to the small collection of artifacts we had received earlier from the dissolution of the Maxfield Parrish Museum. We had delayed accessioning the Parrish objects while we considered whether another museum might be a more logical home for them because they did not "fit" our collection. Once we had accessioned materials just like them in the studio, however, their value as support for our art collection became more apparent. I then defined an artifact collection to accommodate them and other small objects related to works in the art collection that we had acquired over the years.

Yet in my thinking, the museum's permanent collection does not include the studio or artifact collections. If asked the size of the museum's collection, I would report 3,185, not 14,037, counting only the works of art, not the multitude of miscellany in the studio collection. It is, however, an important part of the museum's holdings, vital to the interpretation of the N. C. Wyeth house and studio and held in trust equal to the works of art. We continue to treat objects in the studio collection professionally, conserving them as required, tracking their movements and accounting for them with periodic inventory checks. The Brandywine River Museum is still an art museum, albeit one blessed with fascinating historic structures and artifacts.

From this experience I learned that there is no substitute for clearly thought-out collecting guidelines; however, institutional authorities should judiciously massage and tweak those guidelines when the opportunity to extend and enhance their museum presents itself. I discovered that advances in technology can ease the process of assimilating a large, diverse group of objects. I learned that a registrar must be both flexible and courageous in the face of change. And I learned that a good system of processing objects is a good system, no matter what the objects may be.

Notes

1. Larry Schoonover, *Spokane's Crown Jewel: The Diamond Anniversary of the Eastern Washington State Historical Society, 1916–1991* (Spokane: Eastern Washington State Historical Society, 1991), 2.

2. Hazel A. Burrows at EWSHS, letter to Francine Bonnello, at the Arizona Historical Society, Jan. 15, 1981.

3. Cheney Cowles Museum, "The Auction of Deaccessioned and Non-Relevant Materials." (Spokane: Eastern Washington State Historical Society, 1991).

5. Appendices

Appendix A
MUSEUM UNCLAIMED PROPERTY LAW

Section I: Purpose

The people of this state have an interest in the growth and maintenance of museum collections and in the preservation and protection of unclaimed tangible property of artistic, historic, cultural and/or scientific value left in the custody of museums within this state. Loans of such property are made to these museums in furtherance of their educational purposes. When lenders fail to stay in contact, museums routinely store and care for loaned property long after the loan periods have expired or should reasonably be deemed expired. But, museums have limited rights to the use and treatment of such unclaimed loaned property, all the while bearing substantial costs related to storage, record keeping, climate control, security, periodic inspection, insurance, general overhead and conservation. It is in the public interest to:

   a. Encourage both museums and their lenders to use due diligence in monitoring loans

   b. Allocate fairly responsibilities between lenders and borrowers

   c. Resolve expeditiously the issue of title of unclaimed loans left in the custody of museums

The purpose of this chapter is to establish uniform rules to govern the disposition of unclaimed property on loan to museums and this act should be interpreted with these goals in mind.

Section II: Citation of Law

This law shall be known and may be cited as the Museum Unclaimed Property Act.

Section III: Effective Date

The effective date of this act is _____

Section IV: Definitions

   a. "Lender," -- an individual, corporation, partnership, trust estate or similar organization, whose name appears on the records of the museum as the entity legally entitled to control property on loan to the museum;

   b. "Loan,"- "On loan," or "Loaned," -- property in the possession of the museum, accompanied by evidence that the lender intended to retain title to the property and to return to take physical possession of the property in the future;

   c. "Museum," -- a public or private nonprofit agency or institution located in this state and organized on a permanent basis for essentially educational or aesthetic purposes, which unitizes a professional staff, owns or utilizes tangible objects, cares for them and exhibits them to the public on a regular basis;

   d. "Museum records," -- documents created and/or held by the museum in its regular course of business;

   e. "Property," -- a tangible object, in the custody of a museum, that has intrinsic historical, artistic, scientific, or cultural value;

   f. "Restricted certified mail," -- certified mail that carries on its face, in a conspicuous place where it will not be obliterated, the endorsement "deliver to addressee only" and for which the post office provides the mailer with a return receipt showing the date of delivery, the place of delivery and the person to whom delivered;

g. "Unclaimed property", -- property meeting the following two conditions: (1) property is on loan to the museum; (2) the original lender, or anyone acting legitimately on the lender's behalf, has not contacted the museum for at least 25 years from the date of the beginning of the loan, if the loan was for an indefinite or undetermined period, or for at least 5 years after the date upon which the loan for a definite period expired.

Section V: Museums' Obligations to Lenders

1. Record Keeping for New Loans: For property loaned to a museum on or after the effective date of this act, the museum shall do all of the following at the time of the loan

a. Make and retain a written record containing at least all of the following:

i. The lender's name, address, and telephone number;

ii. A description of the property loaned in sufficient detail for ready identification;

iii. The beginning date of the loan;

iv. The expiration date of the loan.

b. Provide the lender with a signed receipt or loan agreement containing at least the record set forth in subsection (a) above.

c. Inform the lender of the existence of this act and provide the lender with a copy of this act upon the lender's request.

2. Record Keeping for Existing Loans: Regardless of the date of a loan of property, the museum shall do the following:

a. Update its records if a lender informs the museum of a change of address or change in ownership of property loaned, or if the lender and museum negotiate a change in the duration of the loan.

b. Inform the lender of the existence of this act when renewing or updating the records of an existing loan and provide the lender with a copy of this act upon the lender's request.

Section VI: Lenders' Obligations to Museums

1. Notices Required of Lenders: As of the date of this act, the lender or any successor of such lender, shall, regardless of the date of a loan of property in the custody of a museum, promptly notify the museum in writing:

a. Of a change in lender's address; and/or

b. Of a change in ownership in the property on loan to the museum.

2. Documentation establishing ownership: It is the responsibility of a successor of a lender to document passage of rights of control to the property in the custody of the museum.

a. Unless there is evidence of bad faith or gross negligence, no museum shall be prejudiced by reason of any failure to deal with the true owner of any loaned property.

b. In cases of disputed ownership of loaned property, a museum shall not be held liable for its refusal to surrender loaned property in its possession except in reliance upon a court order or judgement.

Section VII: Notice by Museums to Lenders to Terminate Loans for Unclaimed Property

A museum may terminate a loan for unclaimed property in its possession as follows:

1. Good Faith Search: The museum shall make a good faith and reasonable search for the identity and last known address of the lender from the museum records and other records reasonably available to museum staff. If the museum identifies the lender and **the lender's last *known* address, the museum shall give actual notice to the lender that** the loan is terminated pursuant to subsection 2(a) below. If the identity or the last known address of the lender remains unknown after the above described search, the museum shall give notice by publication pursuant to subsection 2(b) below.

2. Notice:

a. **Actual Notice:** Actual notice of termination of a loan of unclaimed property shall take substantially the following form. The museum shall send a letter by restricted certified mail to the lender at the lender's last known address giving a notice of termination of the loan, which shall include the following information:

    i. Date of notice of termination;

    ii. Name of the lender;

    iii. Description of property in sufficient detail for ready identification;

    iv. Approximate initiating date of the loan (and termination date, if applicable), if known;

    v. The name and address of the appropriate museum official to be contacted regarding the loan;

    vi. Statement that within 90 days of the date of the notice of termination, the lender is required to remove the property from the museum or contact the designated official in the museum to preserve the lender's interests in the property and that failure to do so will result in the loss of all rights in the property pursuant to Section VIII of this act.

b. **Notice by Publication:** If the museum is unable to identify sufficient information to send actual notice pursuant to section (a) above, or if a signed return receipt of a notice sent by restricted certified mail under subsection (a) above is not received by the museum within 30 days after the notice is mailed, the museum shall publish the notice of termination of loan containing all the information available to the museum provided in subsection (a) (i–v) above at least twice, 60 or more days apart, in a publication of general circulation in the county in which the museum is located, and the county of the lender's last known address, if known.

Section VIII: Museum Gaining Title to Property; Conditions

As of the effective date of this act, a museum acquires title to unclaimed property, under any of the following circumstances:

a. For property for which a museum provides actual notice to a lender in accordance to Section VII 3(a) above and a signed receipt is received, if a lender of that property does not contact the museum within 90 days after the date notice was received.

b. For property for which notice by publication is made pursuant to Section VII 3(b) above, if a lender or anyone claiming a legal interest in that property does not contact the museum within 90 days after the date of the second publication.

Section IX: Contractual Obligations

Despite this act, a lender and museum can bind themselves to different loan provisions by written contract.

Section X: Effect on Other Rights

a. Property on loan to a museum shall not escheat to the state under any state escheat law but shall pass to the museum under the provision of Section VIII above.

b. Property interests other than those specifically addressed in this act are not altered by this act.

Section XI: Title of Property Acquired from a Museum

A museum which acquires title to property under this act passes good title to another when transferring such property with the intent to pass title.

Section XII: Museum Lien for Expenses of Expired Loans

As of the effective date of this act, a museum shall have a lien for expenses for reasonable care of loaned property unclaimed after the expiration date of the loan.

[From the Old Loans Task Force, Registrars Committee, 1995. Courtesy of the Mid-Atlantic Association of Museums.]

Appendix B

MUSEUM OF HISTORY
Office of the Registrar • 0000 Street, Anywhere, ST 00000
Telephone (000) 000-0000 • Fax (000) 000-0000 • E-mail: registrar@moh.org

AFFIDAVIT

Attach photo of object to back of Affidavit

OBJECT:

Material/Media: **ID Number (if any):**

DIMENSIONS: H.   **W.**   **L.**   **DIA.**   **Weight**

The information supplied in the body of the affidavit should be based on the personal knowledge of the witness'(es) signing the declaration and should include, as thoroughly and to the best of the witness'(es') knowledge:

The witness'(es') connection to the museum, including:

- When the object was seen in the museum for the first time by the witness(es)

- Where the object was seen for the first time by the witness(es)

- The circumstances under which the object was seen

I declare under penalty of perjury of the law that the above-mentioned information is true and correct.

Name and Address of Witness(es)

Signature and Date

[Ed. Note: Courtesy of Melinda Simms]

Appendix C

THE XYZ MUSEUM
53 Xyz Street, Xyztown, Xyzstate 00000
Telephone (000) 000-0000 • Fax (000) 000-0000

INCOMING RECEIPT
For objects placed on deposit for less than six months

The undersigned ("Lender") hereby places the object(s) described herein in custody of The Xyz Museum for the purposes stated, subject to the terms and conditions set forth.

PURPOSE:
_____ Gift or purchase on approval
_____ Loan for exhibition
_____ Research
_____ Other

PROJECT OR EVENT: _____

DATES OF CUSTODY PERIOD: _____

XYZ MUSEUM REGISTRAR: _____

LENDER:
Address:
Telephone: Fax: E-mail:
Contact Person:

OBJECTS: Object/Title/Description/Artist/Medium:

INSURANCE: Total value (estimated fair market value in US $):
Please see reverse
for conditions   The Xyz Museum will insure unless otherwise advised.

SHIPPING METHOD: Incoming:
Return (if applicable):
Date required for receiving item(s):
Date required for return of item(s) (if applicable):
Special instructions for handling, packing, shipping or installation:

SIGNATURE: The Lender acknowledges that he/she has read the conditions above and on the back of this form and that he/she agrees to be bound by them.

Signature:_____   Date:_____
Lender or authorized agent

Signature:_____   Date:_____
For The Xyz Museum

CONDITIONS GOVERNING INCOMING RECEIPT

Care and Handling

1. The Xyz Museum (the "Museum") will exercise the same care with respect to the object(s) on deposit as it does with comparable property of its own.

2. The Museum will not alter, clean or repair objects on deposit without transfer of the object to formal incoming loan status and written approval of lender.

Packing and Transportation

1. The Lender certifies that the objects are in good condition and will withstand ordinary strains of packing and transportation. Evidence of damage to objects on deposit at the time of receipt or while in the Museum's custody will be reported immediately to the Lender.

2. If applicable, objects will be returned packed in the same or similar materials as received unless authorized by the Lender.

3. Costs of transportation and packing will be borne by the Museum unless the loan is at the Lender's request, unless agreed otherwise in advance, or unless lender requests delivery to another location than the original pickup site.

4. International shipments may not be placed on Incoming Temporary Custody, but should be covered by formal incoming loan agreement. Customs regulations will be adhered to in international shipments in this case.

Insurance

1. Unless the Lender expressly elects to maintain his/her own insurance coverage, the Museum's general insurance policy will cover the objects against risks of physical loss or damage from time of release to Museum staff authorized to receive on premises, in the case of delivery by Lender or Lender's agent. If transport is arranged by the Museum, coverage will begin at time of objects' physical release to Museum staff or to professional contract art handling services designated to act as shippers/agents for museum.

2. Insurance will be placed in the amount specified by the Lender, which must reflect fair market value. In case of damage or loss, the insurance company may ask the Lender to substantiate the insurance value. If the Lender fails to indicate an amount, the Museum will set a value for purposes of insurance only for the period of the loan. The Lender agrees that in the event of loss or damage, recovery shall be limited to such amount, if any, as may be paid by the insurer, hereby releasing the Museum and the Trustees, officers, agents and employees of the Museum from liability for any and all claims arising out of such loss or damage.

Reproduction and Credit

1. The Museum assumes the right, unless specifically denied by the Lender, to photograph the objects placed on deposit for documentation purposes only. Photography, videotaping and reproduction for publicity, publication and educational purposes connected with an exhibition or research project must be covered by a formal loan agreement.

Ownership and Change in Ownership

1. The Lender hereby warrants that he/she has full legal title and copyrights to objects placed on temporary custody, or that he/she is the duly authorized agent of the Owner or Owners of them.

2. The Lender will notify the Museum promptly in writing of any change of ownership of the items in custody whether by reason of death, sale, insolvency, gift or otherwise. If ownership shall change during the period of custody, the Museum reserves the right to require the new owner, prior to the return of the work, to establish his or her right to possession by proof satisfactory to the Museum. The new owner shall succeed to Lender's rights and obligations under this agreement, including, but not limited to, the custody period and any insurance obligations.

Custody Period, Extension, Return

1. The objects in temporary custody may remain in the possession of the Museum for the time specified on the reverse, but may be returned to Lender at any time earlier by the Museum. If a time extension is requested by curatorial or administrative staff, for long-term research or further examination prior to acquisition, the transaction will be transferred to a formal incoming loan agreement.

2. Unless the Lender requests otherwise in writing, the Museum will return the items only to the Lender and only at the address specified in this agreement. The Lender shall promptly notify the Museum in writing of any change of address. The Museum assumes no responsibility to search for a Lender who cannot be reached at the address specified in this agreement. The Lender may be required to pay additional costs, if any, if the Lender requests the return of the work to another address.

3. The Museum's right to return the objects from custody shall accrue absolutely at the termination of the loan. If, after two weeks beyond termination of loan date noted above, pursuing all possible means of contact and in accordance with any legal requirements, the Lender cannot be found or the Lender refuses to accept the return of the items on temporary custody, it shall be deemed abandoned property, and become the property of the Museum.

Interpretation

1. This agreement constitutes the entire agreement between the Lender and the Museum and may be amended or modified only in writing signed by both parties. Any changes herein of printed text or written additions must bear the initial of both parties. This agreement shall be governed and interpreted according to the laws of the State of Xyzstate.

2. If the terms of this agreement conflict with the forms, agreements or correspondence of the Lender, the terms of this agreement will be controlling.

Appendix D

THE XYZ MUSEUM
53 Xyz Street, Xyztown, Xyzstate 00000
Telephone (000) 000-0000 • Fax (000) 000-0000

INCOMING DEPOSIT–FOR–STORAGE AGREEMENT

AGREEMENT: The undersigned ("Depositor") hereby places on deposit for storage to The XYZ Museum the object(s) described herein and subject to the terms and conditions set forth.

PROJECT: Storage of:

Dates: Duration of storage:
XYZ Museum Registrar: [Registrar contact information (name, phone, fax, e-mail)]

DEPOSITOR: Depositor:
Address:
Telephone:
Fax:
Contact Person:
E-mail:

OWNER   Owner: For use if owner is different from depositor.
Address:
Telephone:
Fax:
E-mail:

OBJECTS   SEE ATTACHED LISTING (if more than one object)

INSURANCE Total value (estimated fair market value in US $):
Responsibility for insurance (museum, depositor or owner). [Ed. note: stipulate any waivers, additional insured, certificates of insurance required.]

COSTS   Describe any costs and responsible parties, for example: Depositor agrees to reimburse The XYZ Museum for storage as well as preparation and access time. Storage is fixed at $____ per month, payable in four quarterly payments of $____ each. Access and time spent on related projects will be billed quarterly at $____ per hour.

SHIPPING   Identify who is responsible for shipping and what type of shipping is required.

SIGNATURE The Depositor acknowledges that he/she has full authority and power to make this agreement, that he/she has read the conditions above and on the back of this form and that he/she agrees to be bound by them.

Signature:_____Date:_____
       Depositor or authorized agent

Signature:_____Date:_____
       For The XYZ Museum

Please complete, sign and return both copies to The XYZ Museum Registrar. A countersigned copy will be sent to you.

CONDITIONS GOVERNING INCOMING DEPOSIT-FOR-STORAGE

Care and Handling

1. The XYZ Museum (the "Museum") will exercise the same care with respect to the works of art on deposit-for-storage (the "work") as it does with comparable property of its own.
2. The Museum will not alter, clean or repair the work without prior express written permission of the Depositor.

Packing and Transportation

1. The Depositor certifies that the work is in good condition and will withstand ordinary strains of packing, transportation and storage. Evidence of damage to the work at the time of receipt or while in the Museum's custody will be reported immediately to the Depositor. The work will be returned packed in the same or similar materials unless otherwise authorized by the Depositor. Costs of transportation and packing will be borne by the Depositor. Customs regulations will be adhered to in international shipments.

Condition Reports
2. XYZ Museum staff will make initial records and track objects on premises, but will not be responsible for detailed condition checks and condition tracking.

Insurance

The Depositor or Owner of the work is responsible for maintaining his or her own insurance. The Museum must be supplied with a certificate of insurance waiving subrogation against the Museum. If the Depositor fails to supply the Museum with such a certificate, this agreement shall constitute a release of the Museum from any liability in connection with the work. The Museum cannot accept responsibility for any error in the information furnished to the Depositor's insurer or for any lapses in coverage.

Ownership and Change in Ownership

The Depositor will notify the Museum promptly in writing of any change of ownership of the work whether by reason of death, sale, insolvency, gift or otherwise. If ownership changes during the period of this transaction, the Museum reserves the right to require the new Owner, prior to the return of the work, to establish his or her right to possession by proof satisfactory to the Museum. The new Owner shall succeed to Depositor's rights and obligations under this agreement, including, but not limited to, the stated period of deposit and any insurance obligations.

Period of Deposit, Extension, Return

1. The terms of this agreement shall apply to any extension of the period of deposit.
2. Unless the Depositor requests otherwise in writing, the Museum will return the work only to the Depositor and only at the address specified in this agreement. The Depositor shall promptly notify the Museum in writing of any change of address. The Museum assumes no responsibility to search for a Depositor who cannot be reached at the address specified in this agreement.
3. The Museum's right to return the work shall accrue absolutely at the termination of the stated period of deposit. If, after pursuing all possible means of contact, and in accordance with any legal requirements, the Depositor or Owner cannot be found or the Depositor or Owner refuses to accept the return of the work, it shall be deemed abandoned and become the property of the Museum.

Interpretation
4. The above constitutes the entire agreement between the Depositor and the Museum, and may be amended or modified only in writing signed by both parties. Any changes herein of printed text or written additions must bear the initial of both parties. This agreement shall be governed and interpreted according to the laws of the State of Xyzstate.
5. If the terms of this agreement conflict with the forms, agreements or correspondence of the Depositor, the terms of this agreement will be controlling.

Appendix E

53 Xyz Street, Xyztown, Xyzstate 00000
Telephone (000) 000-0000 • Fax (000) 000-0000

STORAGE AGREEMENT RELEASE

THIS Release made this _____ day of _____, 20_____, between Museum A, Inc. (the "Museum") and Party B ("Party B");

WHEREAS, the Museum has provided to Party B storage space on or within property owned by the Museum for the storage of certain paintings, art objects, memorabilia and other personal property owned by or entrusted into the custody of Party B ("Properties");

WHEREAS, Party B has retained the right to withdraw, exchange or add to the number of items constituting the Properties from time to time; and

WHEREAS, Party B desires to hold harmless and indemnify the Museum from and against all liability in connection with any theft, damage or other loss to the Properties, except any such liability resulting from the gross negligence or willful misconduct of the Museum.

NOW, THEREFORE, in consideration of the payment of $_____ and other valuable consideration, receipt of which is hereby acknowledged, Party B hereby agrees to hold harmless and indemnify the Museum from and against all costs, expenses, losses, claims, damages or other liabilities arising out of or in connection with the storage of the Properties on or within property owned by the Museum (including, without limitation, the Museum A building), except (i) any such liability that results from the gross negligence or willful misconduct of the Museum or (ii) as otherwise agreed to from time to time by the parties hereto in Museum Loan Agreements or Receipts or other written instruments.

THE TERMS, covenants and provisions of this Release shall extend to and be binding upon the successors and assigns of the parties hereto.

IN WITNESS whereof, the parties have hereunto set their hands and seals the date first above written.

Museum A, Inc.

By_____Title_____

Party B

_____

[notary public to complete]

Appendix F

53 Xyz Street, Xyztown, Xyzstate 00000
Telephone (000) 000-0000 • Fax (000) 000-0000

DEED OF GIFT

Date: Page_____of _____

Name:

Telephone:

Description of object(s):

Donor hereby transfers and assigns without condition or restriction all right, title and interest free of restrictions or encumbrances in the tangible personal property listed above (the "work"), to The XYZ Museum Association, a corporation existing under the laws of the State of XYZ, for use and disposition by The XYZ Museum Association.

Donor warrants and represents that Donor has the full power and authority to transfer the work to The XYZ Museum Association.

Donor certifies that to the best of the Donor's knowledge, the work has not been exported from its country of origin in violation of the laws of that country in effect at the time of the export, nor imported into the United States in violation of United States laws and treaties.

Donor: _____   Date: _____

Donor: _____   Date: _____

Accepted for The XYZ Museum

by: _____   Date: _____
                     Director

The Donor received no goods or services in consideration of this gift.

See reverse for additional terms

Text for reverse side of DOG

This deed of gift represents an agreement between The XYZ Museum Association and the donor(s) named on the face hereof. Any variation in the terms noted must be in writing on the face of this form and approved in writing by both parties.

Gifts to The XYZ Museum Association are deductible from taxable income in accordance with the provisions of federal income tax law. However, Museum employees cannot, in their official capacity, give appraisals for the purpose of establishing the tax deductible value of donated items. Evaluations must be secured by the donor at his/her/their expense.

Limited gallery space and the policy of changing exhibitions do not allow the Museum to promise the permanent exhibition of any object.

Appendix G

DEED OF GIFT OF FRACTIONAL INTEREST

[Ed. note: This form was developed before the passage of the Pension Protection Act of 2006. It is important, as the regulations are changing quickly, to have an attorney write and approve deeds for gifts of fractional interest.]

I hereby give and deliver to Museum A ("the Museum"), an undivided_____percent (_____%) interest in the work of art described below as an unrestricted gift.:

<artist/maker>
<title>
<description of object>

As owner of an undivided _____percent (_____%) interest in the work of art, the Museum shall be entitled to possession, dominion and control of the property for that number of days during any twelve month period after the date hereof which in sum are equal to the percentage of the Museum's ownership in the work of art. The Museum shall have sole discretion to decide the days during which it shall have possession of the work of art. (The period of initial possession of the property by the Museum shall commence upon the acceptance of this gift by the Museum.)

I give further fractional interests in the work of art in the following fractions, said gifts to be effective on the date(s) specified below:

Fraction	Date
percent (_____%)	beginning January 1, 20_____ and continuing each_____<date>_____of succeeding years.

In the event of my death, then all of the remaining fractions of interest in this work of art shall pass to the Museum at the time of my death.

I understand that it is the purpose of the Museum to promote by all appropriate means a wide public knowledge of and appreciation of fine arts, and I further understand that the management, use, display or disposition of my donation shall be in accordance with the professional judgment of the trustees and director of the Museum.

This deed of gift of fractional interest shall be binding upon my executors, administrators, heirs, and assigns.

Signed and sealed this_____day of _____ , 20_____ .

Witness: By:

_____   _____
witness signature   donor signature

_____   _____
witness name   donor name

                                                  _____
                                                  donor address

                                                  _____

State of

County of

On_____, 20_____ , <donor name>_____
personally appeared before me and acknowledged the foregoing instrument to be his/her free act and deed.

                        <notary signature>_____
                        Notary Public

The Museum hereby accepts the foregoing gift and delivery. The donor received no goods or services in consideration of this gift.

                                          For <Museum Name>

                                          By: _____
                                          museum official signature

                                          _____
                                          museum official name

                                          _____
                                          museum official title

Appendix H

THE XYZ MUSEUM
53 Xyz Street, Xyztown, Xyzstate 00000
Telephone (000) 000-0000 • Fax (000) 000-0000

PROMISED GIFT

The XYZ Museum
53 Xyz Street
Xyztown, Xyzstate 00000

Gentlemen:

I hereby confirm my agreement to give to The XYZ Museum ("Museum"), at or before my death, the work or works of art listed below or on the attachment hereto:

Object Description

You have informed me that other collectors, Trustees and friends of the Museum have indicated their intention of giving to the Museum works of art which they own in order to enhance the Museum's collection. As I believe that definite commitments to make such gifts or bequests will be of great value to the Museum, I have agreed to give the above described work of art to the Museum on the understanding (i) that you will do your best to obtain similar commitments from others and may refer to this agreement in inducing others to make such commitments; (ii) that this agreement shall be governed by the laws of Xyzstate.

I may, according to my own convenience, give this work of art to you during my lifetime. Should this gift not be completed during my lifetime, it is understood that this agreement shall be binding on my heirs, executors and administrators, and that omission from my Will of a specific bequest of this work of art to the Museum shall not release them from delivering the aforementioned work of art to the Museum in accordance herewith, or otherwise impair the force and effect of this agreement.

Neither the Museum nor I shall be under any obligation to insure this work of art during my lifetime. In the event I do not own this work of art at my death because of loss by casualty, the Museum shall have no claim against my heirs, executors or administrators with respect to this undertaking on my part.

I have entered into this agreement on the date indicated below with the full intention that I will be legally bound hereby pursuant to the applicable provisions of the law relating to written obligations and that this agreement shall be binding as well on my heirs, executors, administrators and assigns.

Dated _____   Very truly yours,

_____(Seal)
Name
Address

We confirm the above correctly states the agreement between us.

The XYZ Museum

By: _____   Date:_____

Appendix I

THE XYZ MUSEUM
53 Xyz Street, Xyztown, Xyzstate 00000
Telephone (000) 000-0000 • Fax (000) 000-0000

CO-TENANCY AGREEMENT

This Co-Tenancy agreement is made, as of the latest date indicated on the signature page hereof, by _____ (Museum) and _____ (Co-owner's surname), collectively known as the Parties, regarding the Artist's name, *Title of work*, Date (the "work"), which is owned in undivided fractional shares by the Museum and Co-owner's surname.

RECITALS

a. The Museum is a nonprofit organization that has as one of its principal purposes the encouragement and development of public appreciation of art and the provision of facilities to enable members of the public to observe and study works of art such as the work.

b. The Museum is a tax-exempt organization under Section 501(c)(3) of the Code United States Internal Revenue Code.

c. The parties desire to clarify their respective rights and interests regarding the work.

AGREEMENT

1. **Right to Possession.** With respect to the work, the Museum and Co-owner, respectively, shall have the right to possess and display such work for that number of days out of each 12-month period commencing with the effective date of this agreement (and for each succeeding 12-month period thereafter) as equals 365 days multiplied by the percentage undivided interest held by each of the parties. The parties will mutually agree on the specific days that each will possess the work, but should there be an instance in which agreement cannot be reached, the Museum's preference will prevail.

2. **Right to Dispose of Undivided Interest.** The parties shall each retain the right to sell, give or otherwise transfer all or any portion of their respective fractional undivided interest in the work, provided that any such transferee shall take and hold such interest subject to all of the terms and conditions of this Co-Tenancy Agreement. The parties agree to obtain the written consent of any transferee to the foregoing restriction prior to transferring any interest in the work.

3. **Sale of Entire Work.** Except as otherwise provided herein, neither party may sell the work in its entirety without the consent of the other party. Notwithstanding the foregoing, if Co-owner desires to sell the work to a third party, Co-owner may deliver a written notice (the "Sales Notice") setting forth the proposed third party purchaser and purchase price (the "Sales Price"). The Museum shall then have the right to elect to purchase Co-owner's retained interest in the work for a price equal to the Purchase Price, multiplied by Co-owner's retained percentage interest in the Work. Such an election shall be delivered in writing to Co-owner upon obtaining Board approval, within 30 days following the Museum's receipt of the Sales Notice or at the next regularly scheduled Board of Trustees meeting, whichever represents the longer period of time, but in no event to exceed 90 days. If such an election is made, the Museum shall complete its purchase of Co-owner's retained interest

in the work within 30 days. In the absence of an affirmative election by the Museum to purchase Co-owner's retained interest in the work or in the event the Museum fails to complete the purchase within the designated time period, the Museum shall be deemed to have consented to the sale of the work in its entirety for the Sales Price, and the net proceeds from the sale shall be divided between Co-owner and the Museum based on their respective interests in the work.

4. **Insurance.** The Parties shall at all times keep the work insured at an amount to be mutually agreed between them from time to time. The initial value is $_____. The Museum confirms that while the work is in its possession, and in transit to/from Co-owner, it will be covered under the Museum's fine arts insurance policy. Co-owner confirms that while the work is in Co-owner's possession, it will be covered under insurance maintained by Co-owner.

5. **Income from the work.** The parties shall share any gross receipts that may be derived from the work in proportion to their respective percentage interests in the work.

6. **Identification.** For purposes of Museum records and with respect to identification labels related to the publication and exhibition of the work, the following credit line shall be used: "[Museum], fractional gift of _____."

7. **Conservation.** Each of the parties shall bear their proportionate share of all expenses for necessary cleaning, repairs and similar maintenance of the work that may be required from time to time. The parties shall notify, consult and reach accord with each other before any treatment is undertaken or expenses incurred. Should there be an instance in which agreement cannot be reached, the Museum's preference will prevail.

8. **Preservation.** [For works on paper: Each of the Parties shall ensure that the work is installed in an environment of low light levels (10 foot candles or less is the desired circumstance) and so as never to be exposed to direct sunlight.] Each of the Parties shall ensure that the work is installed or stored in an environment that will not endanger its state of preservation and is handled to the standards of professional art technicians.

9. **Loans.** Any contract for the loan of the work entered into with any third party must be discussed, approved, and signed by all the parties. The Museum will be responsible for managing the loan process in its entirety.

Executed as of the applicable date indicated below.

Date:_____   _____
                                  Museum:

Date: _____   _____
                                  Co-owner:

Appendix J

JOINT OWNERSHIP AGREEMENT

Whereas Museum A (hereafter "A") owns 50 percent and Museum B (hereafter "B") owns 50 percent of a work by Identify Artist (medium, date, height x width in. [height x width cm.]) known as *Title of Work* (hereafter the "work"); therefore, the signatories below hereby agree to the following terms and conditions of their joint ownership:

1. The credit line which shall be used any time the painting is exhibited, published or referred to in print shall be as follows: "Jointly owned by Museum A and Museum B, anonymous gifts."

2. The work shall reside at "B" but be available to "A" for exhibition, occasionally, upon request from "A." To protect the work, "A" shall exercise restraint in requesting the work for exhibition but reserves the right to possession of the work for periods up to eight (8) months of any twelve (12)-month period, unless other arrangements are requested and agreed to in writing. Such exhibition privilege shall be requested at least 60 days in advance and shall be granted without reservation unless the work is an integral part of a special exhibition (as opposed to a routine installation from the "B" collection).

3. Exhibition at "A" shall be made possible without a loan fee charged to "A." "B" may issue a pro-forma loan agreement for the work's exhibition at "A," if desired, and "A" shall issue a certificate of insurance to "B" for the work's value for the exhibition period and related transit. While in the possession of "B," the work may be exhibited at any time at "B"'s discretion without notice to or loan fee charged by "A."

4. "B" shall retain in storage a shipping crate which "A" has paid to have constructed and "B" shall pack the work is this crate without further cost to "A" whenever the work travels to "A" for exhibition.

5. "A" shall arrange round-trip transportation between "B" and "A" and may, at its discretion, transport the work in its crate via an "A" vehicle in custody of at least two (2) "A" staff members.

6. Except in the case of emergency, neither "B" nor "A" shall clean, touch up, reframe, repair or restore the work, nor otherwise change or disturb its physical condition, without the written consent of the other party. Should the work at any time require conservation treatment, both "A" and "B" shall review and comment upon any treatment proposal, and both shall jointly authorize any treatment. The cost of approved treatment shall be borne proportionally as to percentage of ownership interest by "A" and "B" unless treatment is necessitated by damage incurred during loan to a third party, in which case the cost of repairs shall be borne by that borrower. Any difference of opinion as to proper and permissible treatment shall be negotiated and settled by mutual agreement between "A" and "B."

7. "B" and "A" have the right to maintain separate ownership, condition, exhibition, photography and research files regarding the work. For internal purposes of curatorship, registration and scholarship each party may examine and record the work by any modern photographic and nondestructive scientific method. Any activity and/or information about the work generated by either owner shall be copied and reported to the other party and shall not be published without written consent of the other party.

8. "B" and "A" have the right to publish the work, if appropriate license is given by the copyright owner. Each owner shall obtain written permission from the other prior to any publication; such permission shall be granted without reservation, unless extraordinary circumstances intervene. Permissions for

third parties to reproduce the work also shall be subject to joint review and agreement by both parties in writing. Reproduction of the work for commercial profit shall be subject in every respect to joint agreement by "A" and "B," including allocation of expenses, proceeds and net profits from such reproduction.

9. "B" and "A" have the right to lend the work to qualified third parties; however, separate loan agreements must be in place between each owner and the borrower(s) before a loan may proceed. In the case of such a loan request, all expenses of processing, preparation, transportation and insurance shall be borne by the borrower. The crate for the work paid for by "A" may be used in such a loan with the understanding that if it is rendered unusable in any way during the course of the loan it shall be replaced by the borrower. Refusal to lend on the part of either owner shall constitute a rejection of a loan request.

10. While the work is in the custody of either "A" or "B," its entire value shall be covered by a blanket fine-arts all-risks policy maintained by the custodial owner. "A" shall bear responsibility for insurance during transit between the two owners. Net proceeds of any insurance claim (after appropriate credit to either party for out-of-pocket disbursements related to the insurable event; e.g., costs of repair to the work) shall be divided proportionately as to the percentage of ownership interest of each party between "A" and "B." At all times the insurance herein required shall cover the joint interests of both parties, and the policies of insurance shall so specify, naming each party as loss payee according to its percentage ownership. The amount of coverage for purposes of the foregoing obligations to insure the work shall be determined from time to time by the parties hereto. Each party shall keep the other informed from time to time and upon request as to the particulars of its respective insurance of the work and of off-premises insurance coverage by others where required. Any apparent or alleged deficiency in insurance (including the amount of coverage specified herein) shall be negotiated and settled by mutual agreement between "A" and "B." Each party shall bear the total cost of insurance for which it is responsible.

11. When the work is included in any exhibition or other usage not on the premises of either party (including transit and storage periods in connection therewith), the party which was primarily responsible for arranging for such exhibition or usage shall ensure that the work is covered either under the blanket fine-arts all-risks policy of the borrower or under a special policy and shall ensure that all requirements, interest protections, and coverage amounts specified herein are met. Certificates of insurance shall be provided by borrowers to both "A" and "B."

12. Each party shall be liable to the other for a proportional amount, according to the percentage of ownership interest of each, of uninsured loss of or damage to the work caused solely by that party's negligence or by its failure to carry insurance as required herein. Neither party shall be responsible for the protection and safekeeping of the work beyond the exercise of such precautions as are taken for the protection and safekeeping of comparable property of its own, nor assumes responsibility in case of loss or damage due to war, invasion, hostilities, rebellion, insurrection, riot, civil commotion, terrorism, nuclear damage or flood.

13. This Agreement shall be binding upon the parties hereto and upon all successors or assigns.

Signed for Museum B.	Signed for Museum A.
By <name, title>	By <name, title>
Date	Date

Appendix K

INCOMING LOAN AGREEMENT

AGREEMENT The undersigned ("Lender") hereby lends to The XYZ Museum the object(s) described herein for the purposes, and subject to the terms and conditions set forth.

EXHIBITION
Exhibition:
Exhibition Dates:
Loan Dates:
XYZ Museum Registrar:

LENDER
Lender:
Address:
Telephone: (business)   Fax:
Contact Person:
Credit: Lent by _____
                    (Exact wording of lender's name for catalogue, labels and publicity)

OBJECT
Artist/Maker:
Object/Title:
Medium:
Date of Work:

DIMENSIONS Object   height _____in.   width _____ in.   depth _____ in.
                    approximate weight _____ lbs.
May we frame or create mounts if necessary for the safely of the work? _____Yes _____No

INSURANCE
Please see reverse for conditions
Total value (estimated fair market value in US $): _____
The XYZ Museum will insure while on premises unless otherwise advised. Lender is responsible for transport insurance.

Do you prefer to maintain your own insurance?   _____Yes   _____No
If yes, estimated cost of premium:

PHOTOGRAPHY
Please see reverse for conditions
If black-and-white photographs and/or color transparencies suitable for reproduction are available, please state type and where they may be obtained.

SHIPPING/ HANDLING
Date required for receiving loan:
Pick-up and/or return address if different from address above. _____Pick-up _____Return
Address:
Telephone: (business)   (home)
Name of contact if other than Lender:
Please list any special instructions for handling, packing, shipping or installation:

SIGNATURE: The Lender acknowledges that he/she has read the conditions above and on the back of this form and that he/she agrees to be bound by them.

Signature:_____   Date:_____
          Lender or authorized agent

Signature:_____   Date:_____
          For The Xyz Museum

Please complete, sign and return both copies to The XYZ Museum Registrar. A countersigned copy will be sent to you.

CONDITIONS GOVERNING INCOMING LOANS

Care and Handling

1. The XYZ Museum (the "Museum") will exercise the same care with respect to the work of art on loan (the "work") as it does with comparable property of its own.

2. The Museum will not alter, clean or repair the work without prior express written permission of the Lender or except when the safety of the work makes such action imperative.

Packing and Transportation

1. The Lender certifies that the work is in good condition and will withstand ordinary strains of packing and transportation. Evidence of damage to the work at the time of receipt or while in the Museum's custody will be reported immediately to the Lender. The work will be returned packed in the same or similar materials unless otherwise authorized by the Lender. Costs of transportation and packing will be borne by the Museum unless the loan is at the Lender's request. Customs regulations will be adhered to in international shipments.

Insurance

1. Unless the Lender expressly elects to maintain his/her own insurance coverage, the Museum will insure the work wall-to-wall under its fine arts policy against risks of physical loss or damage from external cause while in transit and on location during the period of the loan. The insurance coverage contains the usual exclusions of loss or damage due to such causes as wear and tear, gradual deterioration, moths, vermin, inherent vice, war, invasion, hostilities, insurrections, nuclear reaction or radiation, confiscation by order of any government or public authority, risk of contraband or illegal transportations and/or trade and any repairing, restoration or retouching authorized by the Lender.

2. Insurance will be placed in the amount specified by the Lender which must reflect fair market value. In case of damage or loss, the insurance company may ask the Lender to substantiate the insurance value. If the Lender fails to indicate an amount, the Museum will set a value for purposes of insurance only for the period of the loan. The United States Government Arts and Artifacts Indemnity Act may be applicable to this loan. If so, the Lender agrees to said coverage at U.S. dollar valuation as specified in this loan agreement. If a work which has been industrially fabricated is damaged or lost and can be repaired or replaced to the artist's specifications, the Museum's liability shall be limited to the cost of such replacement. The Lender agrees that in the event of loss or damage, recovery shall be limited to such amount, if any, as may be paid by the insurer, hereby releasing the Museum and the Trustees, officers, agents and employees of the Museum from liability for any and all claims arising out of such loss or damage.

3. If the Lender chooses to maintain his or her own insurance, the Museum must be supplied with a certificate of insurance naming the Museum as an additional insured or waiving subrogation against the Museum. If the Lender fails to supply the Museum with such a certificate, this loan agreement shall constitute a release of the Museum from any liability in connection with the work. The Museum cannot accept responsibility for any error in the information furnished to the Lender's insurer or for any lapses in coverage.

Reproduction and Credit

1. The Museum assumes the right, unless specifically denied by the Lender, to photograph, videotape and reproduce the work for documentation, publicity, publication and educational purposes connected with this exhibition and to produce slides of the work to be distributed for educational use.

2. The work will not be photographed by the general public.

3. Unless otherwise instructed in writing, the Museum will give credit to the Lender in any labels and publications as specified on the face of the agreement.

Ownership and Change in Ownership

1. The Lender hereby warrants that he/she has full legal title and copyrights to the work or that he/she is the duly authorized agent of the owner or owners of the work. The Lender will indemnify, defend and hold the Museum harmless from any losses, damages and expenses, including attorney's fees, arising out of claims by individuals, institutions or other persons claiming full or partial title or copyright to the work.

2. The Lender will notify the Museum promptly in writing of any change of ownership of the work whether by reason of death, sale, insolvency, gift or otherwise. If ownership shall change during the period of this loan, the Museum reserves the right to require the new owner, prior to the return of the work, to establish his or her right to possession by proof satisfactory to the Museum. The new owner shall succeed to Lender's rights and obligations under this agreement, including, but not limited to, the loan period and any insurance obligations.

Loan Period, Extension, Return

1. The work shall remain in the possession of the Museum for the time specified on the reverse, but may be withdrawn from exhibition at any time by the Museum. The Lender agrees that he/she cannot withdraw the work during the period of this agreement without prior written consent of the Museum Director.

2. The terms of this agreement shall apply to any extension of the loan period.

3. Unless the Lender requests otherwise in writing, the Museum will return the work only to the Lender and only at the address specified in this agreement. The Lender shall promptly notify the Museum in writing of any change of address. The Museum assumes no responsibility to search for a Lender who cannot be reached at the address specified in this agreement. The Lender will pay additional costs, if any, if the Lender request the return of the work to another address.

4. The Museum's right to return the loan shall accrue absolutely at the termination of the loan. If, after pursuing all possible means of contact, and in accordance with any legal requirements, the Lender cannot be found or the Lender refuses to accept the return of the work, it shall be deemed abandoned and become the property of the Museum.

Interpretation

1. This agreement constitutes the entire agreement between the Lender and the Museum and may be amended or modified only in writing signed by both parties. Any changes herein of printed text or written additions must bear the initial of both parties. This agreement shall be governed and interpreted according to the laws of the State of Xyzstate.

2. If the terms of this agreement conflict with the forms, agreements or correspondence of the Lender, the terms of this agreement will be controlling.

Appendix L

THE XYZ MUSEUM

53 Xyz Street, Xyztown, Xyzstate 00000

Telephone (000) 000-0000 • Fax (000) 000-0000

OUTGOING LOAN AGREEMENT

The XYZ Museum hereby lends to the borrower identified below the object(s) described herein for the purposes and subject to the terms and conditions set forth.

BORROWER

Borrower:
Address:
Telephone: Fax:
Contact: Title:

OBJECT

Accession Number:
Artist/Maker:
Object/Title:
Medium:
Date of Work:
Dimensions of actual object: with frame or mount:
    Weight (if applicable):
Credit Line (for use in exhibit label and catalog):
Condition:

EXHIBITION

Period of Loan:
Exhibition Title:
Venue(s) and Date(s):

INSURANCE

Insurance value (in U.S. dollars):
_____ To be carried by borrower
_____ To be carried by The XYZ Museum, premium billed to borrower

SHIPPING/ PACKING

Unless otherwise specified, all objects will be released from and returned to:
The XYZ Museum, Receiving Entrance, 53 Xyz Street, Xyztown, Xyzstate.
Special shipping/packing requirements:

DISPLAY

Temperature range: Humidity range: Light levels:
Special display requirements:

SIGNATURE The borrower acknowledges that he/she has full authority and power to enter into this agreement, that he/she has read the conditions above and on the back of this form and that he/she agrees to be bound by them.

Signature:_____ Date:_____
    The XYZ Museum

Signature:_____ Date:_____
    Borrower

Please sign white original and return to The XYZ Museum Registrar. The copy is for your files.

OUTGOING LOAN CONDITIONS

Care and Preservation

Objects borrowed shall be given proper care to insure against loss, damage or deterioration. The borrower agrees to meet any special requirements for installation and handling. The XYZ Museum (the "Museum") certifies that the objects lent are in condition to withstand ordinary strains of packing, transportation and handling. The Museum is to be notified immediately, followed by a full written and photographic report, if damage or loss is discovered. If damage occurred in transit, the borrower will also notify the carrier and will save all packing materials for inspection. No object may be altered, cleaned, repaired or fumigated without the written permission of the Museum, nor may framing, matting, mounting or glazing be changed without written permission; nor may objects be examined by scientific methods without written permission. Objects must be maintained in a fireproof building under 24-hour physical and/or electronic security and protected from unusual temperatures and humidity excessive light and insects, vermin, dirt or other environmental hazards. Objects will be handled only by experienced personnel.

Packing and Transportation

Packing and transportation arrangements for the loan must be approved by the Museum. The borrower agrees to meet any special requirements for packing and shipping. Unpacking and repacking must be performed by experienced personnel. Repacking must be done with either original or similar materials and boxes and by the same methods as the object was received.

Insurance

Objects shall be insured at the borrower's expense for the value stated on the face of this agreement under an all-risk wall-to-wall policy subject to the following standard exclusions: wear and tear, insects, vermin, gradual deterioration or inherent vice; repairing, restoration or retouching processes; hostile or warlike action, insurrection, or rebellion; nuclear reaction, nuclear radiation or radioactive contamination. The Museum shall determine whether the borrower insures the objects or whether the Museum insures them and bills the borrower for the premium. If the borrower is insuring the objects, the Museum must be furnished with a certificate of insurance or a copy of the policy made out in favor of the Museum prior to shipment of the loan. The Museum must be notified in writing at least 30 days prior to any cancellation or meaningful change in the borrower's policy. Any lapses in coverage, any failure to secure insurance and/or inaction by the Museum will not release the borrower from liability for loss or damage.

Reproduction and Credit

The Museum will make available, through an outside service, photographs of objects lent, which may used for catalog, routine non-commercial educational uses, publicity and registrarial purposes. No further use of such photographs can be made and no other reproduction of objects lent can be made without the written permission from the Museum. Each object will be labeled and credited to the Museum in the exact format provided on the face of this contract, both for display labels and publication credits.

Costs

The borrower will assume responsibility for all expenses incurred by the Museum in work by conservators to prepare the object for loan, in packing, crating, transportation, couriers, insurance, photography and any and all other related costs. The Museum will make every effort to provide the borrower with estimates in advance of all applicable costs.

Cancellation/Return/Extension

The loan is made with the understanding that the object will be on view during the entire exhibition period for which it has been requested. Any intention by the borrower to withdraw the loan from the exhibition at any time must be communicated to the Museum immediately. The Museum reserves the right to recall the loan or cancel the loan for good cause at any time, and will make effort to give reasonable notice thereof. Objects lent must be returned to the Museum by the stated return date. Any extension of the loan period must be approved in writing by the Museum Director or his/her designate and covered by written parallel extension of the insurance coverage.

Interpretation

In the event of any conflict between this agreement and any forms of the borrower, the terms of this agreement shall be controlling. For loans to borrowers with in the United States, this agreement shall be construed in accordance with the laws of the State of XYZ.

Additional Conditions for International Loans

Government regulations will be adhered to in international shipments. Unless otherwise stated in writing, the borrower is responsible for adhering to its country's import/export requirements. The borrower will protect objects from possible damage during its customs inspections and will make every effort to ensure that customs examinations are made only on the borrower's premises. If the nature of the material to be exported falls within the types addressed by the UNESCO Convention, its status in the importing country should be verified before this loan agreement is signed by the borrower. The Museum requires a declaration of immunity from seizure if available. The provisions of this loan agreement are subject to the doctrine of force majeure. If U.S. Government Indemnity is secured, the amount payable by indemnity is the sole recovery available to the Museum in event of loss or damage, and objects will be insured in U.S. dollars at their value as of the application date. Current fluctuations affecting value of claims at a later date are not recognized under indemnity.

Bibliography

DOORSTEP DONATIONS

Allen, Thomas B. *Offerings at the Wall*. Atlanta: Turner Publishing Inc., 1995.

Felton, Duery, and Tony Porco. "Mementos and Memories: The Vietnam Veterans Memorial Collection." *CRM*. 18:10 (1995): 30–31.

Moser, Don. "Offerings at the Wall." *Smithsonian Magazine*. 26:2 (May 1995): 54.

Witzig, Katherine Jones. "Collections Management of Abandoned Items at Museums, Memorials and Monuments: Legal, Ethical and Moral Issues." Master's thesis, Seton Hall University, 1999.

GENERAL GUIDES

Buck, Rebecca A., and Jean Allman Gilmore, eds. *The New Museum Registration Methods*. Washington, D.C.: American Association of Museums, 1998.

Dudley, Dorothy H., and Irma Bezold. *Museum Registration Methods*. Washington, D.C.: American Association of Museums, 1958.

Dudley, Dorothy H., and Irma Bezold Wilkinson. *Museum Registration Methods*. 2nd ed. Washington, D.C.: American Association of Museums, 1968.

_____. *Museum Registration Methods*, 3rd ed., revised. Washington, D.C.: American Association of Museums, 1979.

Malaro, Marie C. *A Legal Primer on Managing Museum Collections*. Washington, D.C.: Smithsonian Institution Press, 1998.

Peck, Robert A., and Stephanie Foster. "Legal Title to Art Work Produced Under the Works Progress Administration." General Services Administration, Washington, D.C., 2000. Photocopy.

Phelan, Marilyn E. *Museum Law: A Guide for Officers, Directors and Counsel*. Evanston, Ill.: Kalos Kapp Press, 1994.

Sullivan, Lawrence E., and Alison Edwards. *Stewards of the Sacred*. Washington, D.C.: American Association of Museums, 2004.

HISTORY

Alexander, Edward P. *The Museum in America: Innovators and Pioneers*. Walnut Creek, Calif.: AltaMira Press, 1997.

_____. *Museum Masters: Their Museums and Their Influence*. Nashville, Tenn.: American Association for State and Local History, 1983.

Baas, Jacquelynn, ed. *Treasures of the Hood Museum of Art*. New York: Hudson Hills Press, 1985.

Bandes, Susan J. *Caring for Collections: Strategies for Conservation, Maintenance and Documentation*. Washington, D.C.: American Association of Museums, 1984.

Booth, E. T. *Apprenticeship in the Museum.* Newark, N.J., 1928.

Buck, Rebecca, ed. *History of the Registrars Committee: 25 Years.* N.p.: Registrars Committee of the American Association of Museums, 2002.

Crook, A. R. "The Training of Museum Curators." In *Proceedings of the American Association of Museums [1910 Meeting]*, Buffalo, NY: American Association of Museums, Charleston, S.C., 1911

Dana, John Cotton. *The Newark Museum's Staff*, 1925, Newark Museum archives.

Demarest, Marty. "The Life Above," *Inlander* (Sept. 8, 2005): 27–29.

Guthe, Carl E. *The Management of Small History Museums.* Nashville, Tenn.: American Association for State and Local History, 1959.

Jackson, Margaret Talbot. *The Museum: A Manual of the Housing and Care of Art Collections.* New York: Longmans, Green, 1917.

Jackson, Sidney L. *Libraries and Librarianship in the West: A Brief History.* New York: McGraw Hill, 1974.

Kent, Henry Watson. "Some Business Methods in the Metropolitan Museum of Art." In *Proceedings of the American Association of Museums [1911 Meeting]*, Boston, Massachusetts, Charleston, S.C., 1911.

————. *What I Am Pleased to Call My Education.* New York: Grolier Club, 1949.

Lucas, Frederick A. "The Evolution of Museums." In *Proceedings of the American Association of Museums [1907 Meeting].* Washington, D.C.: American Association of Museums, 1908.

Mann, Virginia. "From Clay Tablet to Hard Disk." In *Registrars on Record*, edited by Mary Case. Washington, D.C.: American Association of Museums, 1995.

Northwest Museum of Arts and Culture. *Campbell House.* Spokane: Eastern Washington State Historical Society, 2005.

Peniston, William, ed. *The New Museum: Selected Writings by John Cotton Dana.* Washington, D.C., and Newark, N.J.: The American Association of Museums and The Newark Museum, 1999.

Rea, Paul M. "Museum Records." In *Proceedings of the American Association of Museums [1907 Meeting]* Washington, D.C.: American Association of Museums, 1908.

Redman, S. J. "What Self-Respecting Museum Is Without One?: The Story of Collecting the Old World in the Science Museum of Minnesota, 1914–1988." *Collections* 1, no. 4 (May 2005): 309–28.

Schoenberg, Wilfred P., S. J. *Indians, Cowboys and Western Art: A History of MONAC.* Spokane: Museum of Native American Cultures, 1981.

Schoonover, Larry. *Spokane's Crown Jewel: The Diamond Anniversary of the Eastern Washington State Historical Society, 1916–1991.* Spokane: Eastern Washington State Historical Society, 1991.

Severance, Frank H. "Historical Museums." In *Proceedings of the American Association of Museums [1910 Meeting]*, Buffalo, NY: American Association of Museums, Charleston, S.C., 1911

Slaughter, Rebecca. *Cooperstown Graduate Program: A Popular History, 1964–2004.* Cooperstown, N.Y.:

Cooperstown Graduate Program, 2004.

Various. *America's Museums: The Belmont Report. A Report to the Federal Council on the Arts and the Humanities.* Washington, D.C.: American Association of Museums, 1969.

_____. *The Organization of Museums: Practical Advice.* Paris, France: UNESCO, 1960.

White, Margaret E. "How A Museum Acquires Objects and Records Them." In *The Journal of the Museum Association of Newark*, New Jersey, 1928.

Wiegand, Wayne A. *Irrepressible Reformer: A Biography of Melvil Dewey.* Chicago and London: American Library Association, 1996.

_____. *Historic Browne's Addition Neighborhood.* Spokane, WA, n.d.

NON-ACCESSIONED COLLECTIONS

Anderson, Gail, ed. *Reinventing the Museum: Historical and Contemporary Perspectives on the Paradigm Shift.* Walnut Creek, Calif.: AltaMira Press, 2004.

Edson, Gary, ed. *Museum Ethics.* New York and London: Routledge, 1997.

Ellis, Judith, ed. *Keeping Archives.* Port Melbourne: Thorpe, 1993.

Gardner, Howard. *Frames of Mind: The Theory of Multiple Intelligences.* New York: Basic Books, 1983.

_____. *Intelligence Reframed: Multiple Intelligences for the 21st Century.* New York: Basic Books, 1999.

Jones, Mark, ed. *Fake? The Art of Deception.* Berkeley and Los Angeles: University of California Press, 1990.

Swartzburg, Susan. *Preserving Library Materials.* Metuchen, N.J., and London: Scarecrow Press, Inc., 1995.

OLD LOANS AND FOUND IN COLLECTION

Anderson, Karen W. "Proposed Institutional Policies and Procedures for Determining Ownership of Collection Materials in the State of Texas." Paper presented at the annual meeting of the Texas Association of Museums, Amarillo, 1995.

Baldwin, Stephanie A. "When Loans Go Bad: 'Good Faith Search' for Missing Lenders in the Information Age." In *Legal Problems in Museum Administration.* Philadelphias: ALI-ABA, 2002.

Benas, Jeanne. "Practical Application of Resolving Old Incoming Loans: A Work in Progress." In *Legal Problems in Museum Administration.* Philadelphia: ALI-ABA, 1992.

Dean, Catherine E. "New Tools for an Old Problem?: Old Loan Research and the Internet." Portions published in *Working Papers, Legal Problems in Museum Administration.* Philadelphia: ALI-ABA, 2002.

DeAngelis, Ildiko. " 'Old' Loans: Laches to the Rescue?" In *Legal Problems of Museum Administration*. Philadelphia: ALI-ABA, 1992.

_____. "Unclaimed 'Old' Loans." Paper presented at the annual meeting of the New England Museum Association, 2004.

DeAngelis, Ildiko, and Marsha S. Shaines. "Giving to Museums: Legal Basics of Donations of Cash, Objects, and Other Property." In *Legal Problems of Museum Administration*. Philadelphia: ALI-ABA, 1999.

Office of the Registrar. "Procedures for Resolving Old Incoming Loans." Office of the Registrar, National Museum of American History, Smithsonian Institution, Washington, D.C., n.d.

Pyle-Vowles, Devon, Chair. "At the Crossroads Are Objects Found in the Collection." Panel discussion at the annual meeting, American Association of Museums, Indianpolis, May 2005.

Simms, Melinda. "Found in Collections: Reconciling Undocumented Objects in Historical Museums." Master's thesis, John F. Kennedy University, San Francisco, 2003.

_____. "'Found in Collections': A Reference Guide for Reconciling Undocumented Objects in Historical Museums." Master's thesis, John F. Kennedy University, San Francisco, 2003.

Tabah, Agnès. "The Practicalities of Resolving 'Old' Loans: Guidelines for Museums." In *Working Papers, Legal Problems in Museum Administration*. Philadelphia: ALI-ABA, 1992.

Teichman, Judith L. "In Support of a Legislative Solution to the Problems of Objects of Uncertain Status in Museum Collections." In *Legal Problems in Museum Administration*. Philadelphia: ALI-ABA, 1983.

_____. "Museum Collections Care Problems and California's 'Old Loan' Legislation." *COMM / ENT: Hastings Communications and Entertainment Law Journal*. University of California. 12:3 (Spring 1990):423-452.

Various. "Resolving Unclaimed Loans Using the Internet: Resources and Case Studies." Paper by graduate students and faculty of the Museum Studies Program, the George Washington University, Washington, D.C., 2002.

Ward, Nicholas. "Cleaning Up Old Loans: Recent Activities." In *Working Papers, Legal Problems in Museum Administration*. Philadelphia: ALI-ABA, 1984.

POLICIES AND PROCEDURES

Gardner, James B., and Merritt, Elizabeth E. *The AAM Guide to Collections Planning*. Washington, D.C.: American Association of Museums, 2004.

Igoe, Kim. "Writing and Updating Collections Management Polices." In *Working Papers, Legal Problems in Museum Administration*. Philadelphia: ALI-ABA, 1997.

Simmons, John. *Things Great and Small: Collection Management Policies*. Washington, D.C.: American Association of Museums, 2006.

SUPPLEMENTARY COLLECTIONS

Baker, Frank C. "School Loan Collections as Prepared by the Chicago Academy of Sciences." In *Proceedings of the American Association of Museums*, 36–43. Buffalo: American Association of Museums, 1910.

Gustafson, Edith, and members of the Lending and Science Departments. *Lending Collections of The Newark Museum*. Newark, N.J.: Newark Museum, 1929.

Hine, Sarah, and Edith Gustafson. *The Lending Department.* Newark, N.J.: Newark Museum, 1928.

WEBSITES

Characteristics of an Accreditable Museum, August 2005: www.aam-us.org

1901–1932: The Income Tax Archives, August 2005: www.tax.org/Museum/1901-1932.htm.

Deardorff's Glossary of International Economics: http://www.personal.umich.edu/~alandear/glossary/d.html.

Lawson, Mary H. "How One Collection Is Getting Its Groove Back: Revitalizing the National Postal Museum's Exhibit and Master and Reference Collection of U. S. Stamps." *EnRoute*, 1998: http://www.postalmuseum.si.edu/resources/6a2t_usstampproject.html

Bannatyne, Leslie. "Striving to Save History's Treasures." *Christian Science Monitor*, (August 2004): http://www.csmonitor.com/2004/0831/p18s02-hfks.html.

Glossary of Smithsonian Institution terminology: http://siarchives.si.edu/collections/tt_acquire.html.

Oakland Museum School Programs: http://www.museumca.org/global/education/schprogguide.html.

THE AUTHORS

Jean Allman Gilmore and Rebecca A. Buck served as co-editors of the AAM Registrars Committee (RC-AAM) journal *REGISTRAR* from 1987 through 1993. They both served as vice-chair then chair of the Mid-Atlantic Association of Museum Registrars Committee (MAAM-RC). They are co-authors of *On the Road Again: Developing and Managing Traveling Exhibitions* (AAM, 2003) and co-editors of *The New Museum Registration Methods* (AAM, 1998). Together they served as presenters in the online continuing professional education program of Georgetown University's museum studies curriculum. They were named co-recipients of RC-AAM's Dudley-Wilkinson Award of Distinction in 2001.

Rebecca A. Buck is chief registrar at the Newark Museum, Newark, N.J. She was formerly registrar at the Hood Museum of Art, Dartmouth College (1982–1990) and the University of Pennsylvania Museum of Archaeology and Anthropology, Philadelphia (1990–1995); and curator of collections at the Cheney Cowles Memorial Museum (Now Northwest Museum of Arts and Culture), Spokane, Wash., from 1975–1982. She holds degrees from Oberlin College and Boston University and teaches in the museum professions program at Seton Hall University. Ms. Buck was awarded the New Jersey Association of Museums' *John Cotton Dana Award* in 2004 and selected for the American Association of Museum's Centennial Honor Roll in 2006.

Jean Allman Gilmore will mark 25 years as registrar of the Brandywine River Museum, Chadds Ford, Pa., this year. She earned a B.A. from Wittenberg University and an M.A. from the University of Wyoming and completed the museum studies program at the University of Delaware. In addition to serving as chair of MAAM-RC, she was co-chair of the MAAM-RC Task Force on Old Loans and secretary of the MAAM Board of Governors.

Index

Page numbers in italics refer to captions or text boxes.